Revival

Glory

"The glory of God is bringing revival, and if we want more revival we must make room for the glory. This is the greatest need of the hour."   Page 239

"Our failure to make room for the glory in our services is the most common reason that the glory is not seen and experienced in church after church across America and around the world. I believe that most of the necessary elements are in place, but we simply don't give God a chance. We don't make room for Him to work. We don't make room for the glory."   Page 239

"It is not for us to say how the glory will affect us. We must make room for God to do in us what He wants."
                                    Page 246

"Prophecy is the voice of revival. Let your prophetic voice bring forth the revival. You'll save yourself thousands of hours of vain activities."   Page 91

"Revival is bringing an acceleration of the purposes of God in the Earth, and an important part of the revival is the revealing to us of our Bridegroom."   Page 281

"If you have been sidetracked by trying a particular method that has borne fruit for someone else, turn back to find the Lord's presence. He is more important than a method, a system, or a program. Come back to the simplicity of His presence "   Page 151

"Under the cloud is the only place of safety. It is the only place of divine health. It is the only place of guaranteed provision. It is the only place of sure revelation. It is the only place which guarantees us salvation for our households and our nation."   Page 151

"When you discover things that seem to contribute to the glory, do those things more; and when you find things that seem to diminish the glory, stop doing them. It's as simple as that."   Page 190

"What hinders us is rarely something complicated. We don't have major problems that need to be overcome, but minor adjustments that need to be made."   Page 240

"It is through the revelation of the Spirit that you will be elevated."   Page 40

"What God wants to do in these last days can only be accomplished in the glory realm."   Page 92

"God's presence is the glory."   Page 132

"Revival is spontaneous, and we must learn to be spontaneous."   Page 152

"There is a rhythm to the glory, and when we speak of the glory cloud, we speak of moving."   Page 155

"Ordinary people are seeing things that only great people knew of in days gone by."   Page 159

Revival Glory

Ruth Ward Heflin

All Scripture references are from the Authorized King James Version
of the Bible, unless otherwise marked.

McDougal Publishing is a division of The McDougal
Foundation, Inc., a Maryland nonprofit corporation dedicated
to spreading the Gospel of the Lord Jesus Christ to as many
people as possible in the shortest time possible.

Published by:

McDougal Publishing
P.O. Box 3595
Hagerstown, MD 21742-3595

ISBN 1-884369-80-4

Printed in the United States of America
For Worldwide Distribution

Dedication

In memory of my beloved brother,
Rev. Wallace H. Heflin, Jr.
(August 24, 1932–December 27, 1996)
whose life touched multitudes with revival glory.

To all of those who have stood with me and supported me in this challenging year.

To all who hunger for revival glory.

In Memoriam

Rev. Wallace H. Heflin, Jr., born August 24, 1932, passed from this life Friday, December 27, 1996. He was a prophet to the nations.

Brother Heflin was born-again on July 5, 1962 and began immediately serving the Lord with zeal. He first traveled with his father, doing tent meetings throughout Virginia and North Carolina and pastoring the Calvary Pentecostal Tabernacle in Callao, Virginia. Then he began traveling the nations of the world, training men and women who today move in similar prophetic anointing throughout the earth. Although he ministered to more than one hundred and fifty nations, he had a special burden for Israel, China and Russia and ministered with teams in those countries at least once a year. He was a dynamic evangelist with an outstanding healing and miracle ministry. Many knew him simply as "The Miracle Man."

Upon his father's death in 1972 he became co-pastor (with his mother) of the Calvary Pentecostal Tabernacle in Richmond, Virginia, co-director of the Calvary Pentecostal Campground in Ashland and the overseer of existing satellite churches. Under his leadership and guidance, the ministry his parents established in 1937 has greatly multiplied in size and outreach and has touched every nation of the world.

Brother Heflin's life and ministry has reached hundreds of thousands of people around the world. He was an apostle and father in the faith who encouraged hundreds of men and women to enter the ministry and to step out into a deeper life of faith. He was uniquely generous, and encouraged many others to give their way out of poverty. He had a beautiful prophetic gift and was tireless in ministry, giving all his strength to the Lord and to the people – until the end. He leaves behind a prophetic example in this unique time in which we live. He has already laid his hat at Jesus' feet and is even now in the war room of Heaven, looking over the plans for Triumphal Reentry and his rightful place as general in God's army.

About the Title

One night at our camp, as we were singing spontaneously, one of the sisters began to sing a phrase over and over again about revival glory. We had been working on a sequel to *Glory*, and at one point I had thought of calling it *The Cloud of Glory Is Moving* because of a particularly powerful chapter on that subject, but I wasn't sure that was the right title for the book. I was trusting God to show us the correct one. There it was, coming out of the river, flowing to us supernaturally, *Revival Glory*. The title came forth from the flow of the river.

Contents

Introduction

When my brother, Rev. Wallace H, Heflin, Jr., passed away in December of 1996, I received the news by telephone in my hotel room in Burkino Faso, in the central part of Africa. It was many hours before I could get a flight back to America, and while I waited alone in my hotel room, one verse of scripture repeatedly went through my spirit: *"upon whom the ends of the world are come"* (1 Corinthians 10:11). I knew that my brother's homegoing was because the coming of the Lord was at hand. I felt God's time clock accelerating and knew that God would use my brother's passing to challenge many people not only to be ready for His coming but to get on with the work of the harvest because time is short.

The next several days proved this to be true, as large numbers of ministers, both American and foreign, passed by his casket to pay their respects to a man who had blessed their lives, and I could see that they were greatly stirred by his passing. At that time I sensed some of the negative events that would shortly come upon the face of the Earth.

Yesterday morning, nearly a year later, in the Sunday morning service in Richmond, I suddenly remembered again the same scripture: *upon whom the ends of the world are come*. This time I felt the positive aspects of the verse and I sensed the great responsibility we have on our shoulders to bring in the last-day revival in all its glory and magnificence. I know that we have the God-given ability to bring in the final harvest.

God has used my book *Glory* to cause many of the questions people had concerning what God is doing in the present revival to fall away. Pastors are buying the book to give to their staff members so that they can move into the revival. I am pleased with the response it has received.

Another of the things *Glory* is doing for people is opening the horizons of their souls. Numerous people have written to me and said God was doing some of these things in their lives, but they had nobody as a frame of reference to know if it was God. They said, "Because we had no frame of reference, we didn't know anybody to speak to, and we didn't want people to think we were going off the deep end, we didn't tell anybody and we didn't pursue it."

In recent years, as we sought God and moved into the glory, we have learned and experienced so much more that I am constrained to write a second volume. This book will lead those who are genuinely hungry for revival into a deeper revelation of what God wants to do in this time.

This is a time of revival, for which I feel uniquely prepared. I was born in revival, grew up in revival and have been privileged to pioneer revival in many parts of the world. I have witnessed the outpouring of the Spirit now through many decades and have a very great consciousness of what revival glory is. I cannot remember a time that I was not blessed by a measure of revival and a measure of the glory. Now, God is taking us all into greater glory, *Revival Glory*.

Ruth Heflin
Ashland, Virginia
November 24, 1997

Revival Glory

Chapter 1

Our Call to Revival

It is a light thing that thou shouldest be my servant to raise up the tribes of Jacob, and to restore the preserved of Israel: I will also give thee for a light to the Gentiles, that thou mayest be my salvation unto the end of the earth. Isaiah 49:6

Before my brother passed away, at the end of December 1996, God had spoken to me that I would be spending more time in America in 1997. I knew that I was coming to help with the breaking revival in America but didn't realize that the Lord was already preparing us for what was to come in our own family and ministry.

I had been out of America in ministry for the better part of thirty-nine years and had only returned at campmeeting times. I learned to do a lot that the average American never learns to do, as I traveled in many foreign countries. But now I was coming home and had to learn about some of our modern conveniences. For instance, I had never used an ATM card.

Jerusalem has a small town atmosphere and I knew everyone there. As I was walking down the street, if I decided I wanted to buy a newspaper, someone would give it to me and let me pay them later. "I didn't bring my purse with me this morning," I would say. "Would you mind? I'll have someone bring you the money." I was never refused and never asked to sign anything. Now I had to learn a whole new way of life. When I presented a check here, I was asked for two different forms of identification to prove who I was. It's another world.

Not many people knew me around America, but God began to drop America more and more into my spirit. Even Cindy Jacobs had called me out at a meeting in September of 1996 at CBN's Revivalfest at the Founder's Inn in Virginia Beach, Virginia. God said through her, "Daughter, come home. You are needed in America."

Then, when I was invited to speak at a Pastor's Conference at the Brownsville Assembly of God Church in Pensacola, Florida, enough pastors put their cards in my hand and asked me to come to their churches to keep me busy until Jesus comes. Many of those pastors wrote on the back of their cards how many members they had, thinking that this would be a good inducement to get me to come: eighteen hundred, twenty-five hundred, five thousand.

I was not about to start making decisions that way. I was determined to continue to move by the voice of the Spirit. God blessed our family when we had a little storefront church in Richmond, Virginia, when I was a child, and sent someone to help bring revival to us, and I could never forget that help. I was ready to go to the storefronts, if that was what the Lord wanted. I had pioneered revival in many parts of the world, and I was ready to pioneer again.

I had already arranged my ticket to be in America for the New Year's Eve service. I thought that if God was going to use me in America for revival in 1997, I should be there for that service to hear what God was saying prophetically at our church in Richmond about the coming year and what He was saying about America. This service is always one of the highlights of the church's calendar year and people come from far and wide to hear what God is saying. I knew that this would only be a beginning, for it was, for me, a declaration of my faith in what God had told me about my coming ministry in America.

When I got word of my brother's sudden death, I was in Africa. I had just one day left of my scheduled ministry there, and I would be flying to Virginia. Instead of arriving on the 31st, as I had planned, I was forced to fly back one day earlier to make funeral arrangements.

Right after the funeral, I flew back to Israel. We had had been invited by the Prime Minister of Israel, the Speaker of the Knesset and the Mayor of Jerusalem to be present at the Knesset for the last event in connection with the three-thousand-year anniversary of King David. I had planned that a long time before. After that event, however, I immediately flew back to the States to be here in time for our annual worker's convention.

I arrived late the night before, and the next morning as we started the meetings, a prophetic word came forth in which the Lord said, "I will give you the pattern of what to do." As this word was given, I suddenly saw both of God's hands on a gossamer fabric which He was dropping down from Heaven. On it was an outline of the United States. Lights began to come on all across America on the banner until there was not a city, town or village where the light could not be seen. I knew I had seen the pattern of the coming revival, and I turned to those who were involved in the ministry and said, "God said that the pattern would be America."

This was a dramatic change for all of us, as the campground in Virginia had been, for many years, a training center for those who felt led to serve God among the nations of the world. Most of our ministry had been outside the United States. My brother took fifty-five ministry tours to Israel and, in recent years, took groups to Russia twice a year for evangelism and church planting, as well as yearly trips to China and occasional trips to Nigeria, Brazil, India, the Philippines, Tibet and many other countries. In all, he had preached in nearly a hundred countries and my mother, Rev. Edith Ward Heflin, in about eighty. Many of our staff and associates had preached in twenty-five nations or more.

The Lord was very gracious to me in this regard. I had been to every nation I knew of except North Korea. Miraculously I went to North Korea, with Senator Stewart Greenleaf of Pennsylvania and his delegation of ten, and returned in early December, just two weeks before my brother's death. So before God moved me into a ministry to all of America, He opened to me the last remaining nation that I had not been able to visit.

Like everyone in a new position, I wanted to do those things that we had been doing in the past. I was determined to keep all the existing programs going and to add new ones. My brother had been so blessed in his mission trips and, since he had already announced a trip to Israel for March and a trip to Russia for April, I said that we would take those trips and had asked Brother Jones to be the host for them.

The week before the presidential inauguration in Washington, D.C., in 1997, we were busy preparing for the Presidential Inaugural Prayer Breakfast that I was hosting at the Sheraton Hotel. The nights that we didn't have church services in Richmond we were at the campground praying. We sang prophetically and were carried away in the Spirit. During this intense time of revelation, the Lord suddenly made me to know that it would not be a problem for us to keep taking the missions trips, just as we had been doing. If we insisted on continuing all the outreaches to Russia and the other countries, we could do it. We had

the skill and ability to do it and the personnel to accomplish it. He showed us, however, that we didn't
have the time for it. He wanted us to now give our
time and strength to the revival in America.

Brother Dwight Jones had been in the habit of going twice a year to Israel with my brother and on
several trips to Russia. I told him to feel free to take
groups to those places, but that we would not be having time for this ministry. I removed the tours from
our flyers which announced all our upcoming events.
We left the Women's Convention and the Men's Convention, the Summer Campmeeting, and the Winter
Campmeeting on the flyers, but we took off the trips
in March and April, for God had shown us a new
pattern.

This seems like such a simple thing in the retelling,
yet it is surprising how locked in we get to ministry
patterns. This changing pattern remains a bone of contention with some people until now, but revival means
change.

One night during that same winter campmeeting,
when Brother Clark Taylor was speaking, I saw a vision of some cornfields and a lone country house in
the middle of them. The Lord said to me, "The heart-
land of America." For some years, I had been jetting
from big city to big city, all over the world, and it
seemed odd that suddenly the Lord would bring me
back to America and show me a cornfield and one
country house in the middle of it. But I was willing.

Not long afterward I received a telephone call from a pastor inviting me to Paris, Illinois. "Are there cornfields there?" I asked.

She laughed and said, "There is nothing but cornfields here."

"Then I'll come," I told her and I explained why.

While I was in Paris, Illinois, I met a pastor who had a church right in the middle of a cornfield. He was very receptive to our ministry.

Most of the churches I have been led to minister in this year have been in towns of less than two thousand people. The total population of the town was less than the membership of many of the larger churches to which I was invited. But God had chosen to send me to the heartlands, and I was loving every minute of it.

The revelation we receive may not always be the one we want, but if we preach it we have to live by it. I had no great desire to go to the cornfields, but God knows where He needs us. Each of us has our "druthers." Some people even get out their prophecies and try to choose the one they think is best to believe for, but that's not the way it works.

You can't pick and choose. You can't plan and arrange. You can't organize. You can't manipulate. Christ is Lord. If He shows you the heartland of America with a cornfield, you need to ask someone where the cornfields of America are. Somehow I had never pictured myself in middle America, but when the Lord showed me the cornfields, I got ready to go there.

When God speaks to you to go somewhere, you can know that someone in that place is praying. It may be an individual or a church, a government official or a whole group of people. Someone is praying the Macedonian prayer: *come over and help us.*

Are you willing to become the answer to that prayer? When we are able to tell the story of the heart-land of America, there will be much to tell, the unfolding of the plan and purposes of God. This is God's day. It's His hour for revival in America and the ingathering of the harvest. We know that God will still send us to the nations, but, for the time being at least, we are committed to revival right here at home.

Perhaps none of this should have surprised me. God had awakened me one night in Jerusalem, and I heard His voice saying, *"From sea to shining sea."* As I struggled to get fully awake, I was trying to remember which of our patriotic songs contained that phrase. Before long, it began to come to me:

> *America, America.*
> *God shed His grace on thee.*
> *And crown thy good with brotherhood,*
> *From sea to shining sea.*

When God gave us the pattern for America, we had no details. We had to learn as we went.

Earlier in 1996, my brother and I and Dwight Jones, our friend from Texas, had been talking one day about the revival coming to America, and we agreed that we needed to begin to do in America what we had been doing overseas for many years. We had in mind to do one major meeting somewhere in America every month. Before he died, my brother had already planned such meetings in Louisiana and Texas, and, after his passing, Brother Jones and I felt led to go ahead with those scheduled meetings.

God gave us the free use of an auditorium for the first meeting. It was a Union Hall in New Orleans and belonged to the Steam Fitter's Union. I didn't know that the Steam Fitter's Union still existed, but I appreciated the free use of their auditorium and the gracious reception we were given. New Orleans was a lovely place to begin our ministry in the United States. Everyone there was very responsive to us.

In most cities, you can pay five hundred to a thousand dollars a night to use even small halls, and if you are just starting out, that's a major consideration. Brother Jones has a lovely conference center in Caddo Mills, just outside of Greenville, Texas, that he bought within the past few years, and we decided to have the second meeting there. It is fifty miles or so south of Dallas, in the plains of Texas.

About ten days before we got there, Brother Jones was getting ready to put a few announcements on television. Then, Rev. Floyd Lawhon who was in Atlanta,

Georgia, called Marcus Lamb, the owner of Channel 29 in Dallas and said, "I've been reading a book called *Glory*. Let me read an excerpt to you from the post-script," and he read my statement that when revival in America is in full bloom, the Dallas Metroplex will be the center of the revival. Marcus Lamb was so excited that he quoted the statement on television daily for sometime. He ordered a thousand copies of my book and challenged his listeners to get their own copy. When he discovered that I was coming to town, he arranged for Brother Dwight Jones and me to be on one of his programs. God had been using him for revival.

He interviewed us for an hour about revival and played it back three times that day and many times over the days and weeks to come. Since then I have returned as a guest on Channel 29 in Dallas several times. Brother Lamb and his wife Joannie are busy promoting revival all over the Dallas–Ft. Worth Metroplex and graciously brought the mobile television unit and a crew out to Caddo Mills and filmed two services for us.

Brother Buford Smith of Abingdon, Virginia, pre-empted everything in his television schedule for five hours, as we talked about revival two nights in succession.

When God makes His winds blow, He can quickly make room for those who know the wheel within the wheel turning, the fire within the fire burning, the glory of God being revealed in this day and hour by the Spirit of the Lord.

A pastor called me from North Carolina. Someone from Atlanta had read my book and sent him a copy. He read it and began to experience violent shaking in his body. Before long, great revival had come to his church. Before I finished talking with him that day I felt revived myself. It was wonderful what was happening to him and his people.

We are going to experience the shaking of which Ezekiel spoke, and we are going to experience the coming together as well. As people everywhere reach out to God, we will be increasingly joined one to the other. When the pastor called, I didn't even ask him what denomination he was. It doesn't matter. I never ask. If people want to mention that they are Methodist or Baptist or Presbyterian, that's up to them. I don't care. It's totally immaterial. They are bones that are coming together in this last day and hour, "bone to his bone." This is part of revival.

We are about to see even greater things. And how will God do such a great work so quickly? I am reminded of what God did through Rev. T.L. Osborn many years ago in Mombasa, Kenya. When he held his great crusade there, a thousand new congregations were raised up in the year following the crusade. The crusade itself lasted only about a week, yet God so stirred the local brothers that an amazing work was accomplished in a short time.

Rev. Mattson Bose, a wonderful Swedish pastor from Chicago, was used of God to further the revival. He would fly into Africa for two weeks of faith clinics where he gathered all the African brothers and taught them the basic principles of healing the sick, casting out devils, and winning the lost. Six months later he would bring them together again and teach them some more. This resulted in the establishment of strong and stable congregations. This same thing was repeated in many other places as the revival fires spread from place to place, and God is going to do it again, just as quickly.

God is doing an amazing thing in raising up the new converts of Asia, South America, Africa and the former Eastern Bloc countries. He is giving them on-the-job training. Some very young pastors in Russia, men who have been saved only a short time, have stepped out and done amazing things. They might not have all the answers we would like them to have, but some of them have become very successful in the Kingdom of God. God's fire is burning within them. They're seeing the purposes of God fulfilled in their lives, and they're learning on the job.

In Russia today a convert of only a few months time sometimes becomes pastor of a sizable congregation. They don't know yet about all the various doctrinal viewpoints, yet they are being used of God to bless many thousands of people. We are going to see a great increase in this phenomenon.

Oh, how exciting! God can do a quick work when we give Him the opportunity. We are about to see the most amazing things we have ever seen. God is teaching us on the job, and I am so glad that I have been given a part in the harvest.

Our Heavenly Father,

We speak revival fire, glory fire, into the souls of all who read this. I declare such a stirring up within, a stirring up unto revival and the taking hold of the same with all that is within and that we will not let go until revival is in our land, from sea to shining sea.

In Jesus' name,
Amen!

Chapter 2

Lifted Up for Revival

*And the Gentiles [the nations] shall come to thy
light, and kings to the brightness of thy rising.*
Isaiah 60:3

God's plan is always a man. When He is about to
do great things, He finds someone through whom He
may do it. His choosings are not as man chooses:

*For ye see your calling, brethren, how that not
many wise men after the flesh, not many mighty,
not many noble, are called: But God hath chosen
the foolish things of the world to confound the
wise; and God hath chosen the weak things of the
world to confound the things which are mighty;
And base things of the world, and things which
are despised, hath God chosen, yea, and things
which are not, to bring to nought things that are:
That no flesh should glory in his presence.*
1 Corinthians 1:26-29

When God lifts us up, there is no struggle. When
God does a thing, it is done well. When God does the

work, it will last. You may not have to take a tiny step at a time until, at last, you reach the top. Get in the Spirit and you will find yourself quickly being lifted to the top.

If we are willing to lift up our eyes, God will lift us up. If we are willing to respond to that heavenly pull, He will lift us up. The needs of revival demand it.

I didn't know that my brother would pass away at the end of 1996, necessitating my moving to Virginia from Jerusalem to assume his ministry, but God had been telling me "I will lift you up." My book *Glory* had been out for several years and it had already blessed many, but I was still relatively unknown in America since I had spent most of my time in Hong Kong, in Israel and other countries.

Then, suddenly I was invited to speak at the Pastor's Conference in Pensacola, Florida, and, after that, at two more such conferences there. In those three conferences alone, I ministered to approximately six thousand pastors.

I was invited, along with my brother, to the Revivalfest, hosted by the 700 Club and CBN, at the Founders Inn in Virginia Beach, Virginia, two years in a row. There we ministered prophetically to many people. One of them was Oral Roberts.

It was a wonderful word that the Lord gave him, and the opening sentence set the tone: "Your greatest days are just ahead." In the natural, that seemed like a strange word because his son Richard had more or

less indicated the night before that his dad had re-
tired and moved to California, but God was saying
something else.

When I finished prophesying, Brother Roberts said
something to the effect that he didn't have a word of
knowledge ministry like Richard, and you could tell
he was feeling a little awkward because of it. My
brother spoke up and said, "There's not one person
in the world who wouldn't be thrilled to have Oral
Roberts lay his hand on their head." He was encouraging Brother Oral Roberts to use what God had given
him.

Afterward Brother Roberts began to tell me what
he was doing in connection with television, and I
could see what God meant by saying that his greatest
days were still ahead. Recently, when I turned on the
television, I saw Brother Oral Roberts preaching at
Brother Rod Parsley's church, and my how blessed I
was to see how well he was doing. He looked to me
as if he were twenty years younger, and he was moving out among the people in a way I had never seen
him do before. I knew that God's word to him was
being fulfilled in a very special way. It really doesn't
matter how old we are. When God has ordained us
to help bring in revival, He will do the work.

I was unable to stay for the full Revivalfest that first
year and had to leave early to return to Jerusalem.
My brother stayed on, and that night was invited to
have dinner after the evening service with Pastor

Benny Hinn. When Jackie Yockey, Guest Coordinator for the 700 Club, introduced him to Benny Hinn, Benny said, "I know your sister in Jerusalem. She prophesied over me many years ago that God would use me among the leaders of the world and would give me the ministry in which I am now flowing. Some of the things she prophesied are just now beginning to come to pass, and she said all these things years before I came into prominence."

The next day my brother called me to tell me what had been said. My first response was, "I never prophesied over Benny Hinn," thinking of the Benny Hinn we all know now.

My brother continued, "Jackie asked him, 'Was that when you were still wearing a pony tail?' and he said it was. She asked, 'Was that when you were still stuttering?' and he said it was." The experience had been so life-changing for him that he had often told it to his staff, and they knew the detail of it well. Through the years, however, I had prayed over so many people that I couldn't remember it.

"Well, he has never forgotten it," my brother said. "He is grateful and wants to see you in person to tell you." When we did meet again, Benny gave me an open invitation to be with him in his great crusades, and I have taken him up on that invitation whenever I have had free time. I attended meetings in Oslo, Norway; Richmond, Virginia; Raleigh, North Carolina; Atlanta, Georgia; and Miami, Florida, and each time Brother Benny has graciously honored me publicly.

In three simple events God seemed to wipe out the obscurity of the past thirty-nine years of ministering overseas to facilitate my reentry into American society.

Suddenly my book *Glory* was in great demand, was on the Christian best-seller list, was moving into its seventh edition in English and was available in French, Spanish, German, Swedish, Finnish, Russian, Norwegian, Korean, Latvian and several Indian dialects, and was in the process of being translated into many other languages.

All it took was three events for God to begin to do what He said He would do, to make my name more widely known and to open doors more fully to me. I soon found that I had far more invitations than I could possibly fill.

We often see the limitations, when we should be seeing the miraculous provision of God. All He has to do is send a wind our way and, in a moment's time, the necessary changes are taking place. Overnight we go from glory to glory, from one open door to the next.

One morning recently while preaching in Texas I saw a vision of satellite television and began to immediately speak and declare that God would put me on satellite television soon. That afternoon I received an invitation to preach at the Breakthrough Revival Explosion at Trinity Music City in Hendersonville,

Tennessee, where God has been sending revival, and where TBN has been telecasting revival to the nation and the world. The date has not been set, but expect it to be soon. I am excited about the opportunity as in one single telecast I will preach to more people than in my entire life.

And this is only the beginning. The days just ahead will be the greatest for all of us.

How will God do it? I don't know, but I'm not worried about it. He is Sovereign Lord, and He can do exactly what He wants to do, anytime He wants to do it. My confidence is in Him.

In the story of Esther and Mordecai, the wicked Haman was plotting to destroy the people of God, but God caused King Ahasuerus not to sleep one night. He felt compelled to get up and examine the chronicles. There he discovered the name of Mordecai, a man who had done good and had never been rewarded for it.

The next morning, as early as possible, the king felt compelled to send someone to find Haman and bring him to the palace. "What would you do," he asked Haman, "for a man who deserves to be honored?"

Haman was sure he must be the man, so he spoke greater things than he would ever have dared to say otherwise. "That's good," the king replied. "I want you to do all those things you have said for a man named Mordecai whom you will find, I am told, sitting in the gate." God knows how to turn every bad intention aside and to cause the wheel of God to favor your life. He has no limitations.

Our Sovereign Lord doesn't need to be awakened in the night to show anyone how to honor you. He never sleeps. He knows how to put it into the spirit of someone who hasn't thought about you in a long time to call you on the telephone, and, before you realize it, a whole process has been put into motion. There's a wind blowing all across the land, a wind of God's favor.

We must rise to the challenge of the moment. It would be terrible to stand on a great platform without having a greater glory in our lives to bless others. God must enlarge us and place that greater glory within us, so that when opportunities come to us, we will be able to present the excellent glory He is bringing forth in this day and hour.

Stop looking to the temporal, and start seeing the eternal. Stop squandering all your prayer time on things that will pass away and start believing God for things that will last forever. Some of us are guilty of fasting and praying to keep the very things God wants us to let go. We're trying to get more strength to hold on to what we have, while God is trying to get us to let loose. We keep grasping things tighter and tighter, while He's trying to get us to let them go.

Not only will we not look to temporal things in the days ahead, we won't even consider them. We will be so consumed with the eternal realm that temporal things will seem as nothing to us.

We can no longer afford to live only in the natural realm. We must live in the supernatural. Let yourself soar away and be changed from glory to glory. Receive greater and greater glory, greater and greater revelation, greater and greater insight, greater and greater provision.

Let the hastening of the Spirit be felt down deep in your spirit. We are hastening unto the coming of the Lord, hastening unto the fullness of His purposes.

It is through the revelation of the Spirit that you will be elevated. You will no longer move up a step at a time. You will suddenly go from the bottom step to the top step. You will suddenly move up from the lower floors to the upper floors. Don't stand by and watch as others are lifted up. It's also you that the Lord wants to lift up.

When I was a child I was blessed to be able to skip a couple grades in school. When we moved and I went to a new school the teachers would decide that I was too big to be in the class I was presently in and wanted to move me up. They asked me and my parents if we thought it was okay, and we thought it was wonderful. Whereas most of my classmates were seventeen or eighteen when we graduated, I could have graduated at fifteen. I decided to prolong my studies a few months longer and actually graduated at sixteen. God will let you skip some grades, too. He'll let you skip some steps and move on up into His glory. Be lifted up for revival.

There has always been one book that was a key to each revival. Back in the fifties, Gordon Lindsay, the founder of Christ For the Nations in Dallas, Texas, wrote a wonderful book about the revival brought in with the ministry of Brother William Branham. It was called *A Man Sent From God.* I was about ten at the time and had recently been filled with the Spirit. We were living in a little parsonage over our church on Hull Street in Richmond, Virginia, and I will never forget the days that Mother and Daddy and I would sit together in the sitting room adjoining the kitchen. A great light was coming in through the windows as Mother read to us aloud from that book.

As she read the story of what God was doing in Brother Branham's life and ministry, we all three wept. Occasionally, she was overcome with emotion and stopped reading for a moment. She couldn't help but notice that Daddy and I were crying just as hard as she. Then, after a few moments, she would read on, and we would all cry some more. We were thrilled because God was answering our prayers and sending revival to our nation.

The book stirred people all across America. They had already experienced a measure of spiritual hunger, but the telling of the wonderful works of God put an even greater hunger into their spirits, and the result was great revival across this country. I remember it well. We had meetings every night in our church for five years, with all-night prayer meetings every Friday night.

In the sixties, God used two books to bring revival. John Sherrill, Senior Editor of Guidepost Magazine, had a hand in writing both of them. His book *They Speak With Other Tongues* was actually the first commercially published book to document the outpouring of the Holy Ghost down through the centuries. It particularly emphasized what God was doing at that moment, and it made people everywhere hungry for more of God. God used it to spearhead what later became known as the Charismatic movement, as large numbers of pastors and missionaries from the historic churches were baptized in the Holy Ghost.

John Sherrill also wrote, with David Wilkerson, the powerful *The Cross and the Switchblade*, the story of David's intervention in the drug scene of New York streets where large numbers of gang members were saved and stayed saved because they discovered the power of the Holy Ghost to keep them. That book reached out all over the world and touched hungry hearts in every major Christian denomination and group and was largely responsible for the revival of the sixties.

Since that time, I know of no single book that has affected such a large number of people for revival. There have been many good ones. One of my favorites is *Angels On Assignment* by Charles and Francis

Hunter. I have read it and reread it, and I get blessed every time. The experiences of Pastor Roland Buck will lift any sincere believer into the heavenly realms. In general, though, I would say there hasn't been another book that has so shaken God's people worldwide.

When I was preparing to write *Glory*, God told me that it would be such a book, and the letters that pour in from those who have read it seem to prove the fulfillment of His promise to me. The effects people describe to me sound very much like what happened to me as a girl when Mother read to us from *A Man Sent From God*. God is fulfilling His promise to me that He would use my book to help bring in the last-day revival.

Recently I received a fax from Jerusalem stating that a Kenyan brother who was attending an international conference on the environment in Netanya attended our daily prayer meeting in Jerusalem the day before. In Kenya he had read a photocopy of my book *Glory*. He said that no one seemed to know who had the original copy as everyone was reading photocopies. He felt he had to find our place of ministry in Jerusalem and did so with great effort. Our telephone had not been working for about a week, yet he wanted to tell us how much the Kenyans were being blessed by the book.

The same day I received another fax, this one from a mission in a remote part of Chile. The members of the church took turns reading the one copy of Glory they had (in Spanish), and they were so hungry for more that they were inviting me to come and teach them.

When I was in Oslo, Norway, in May 1997 I was aware that even in the Pentecostal and Charismatic churches revival was several years away. I knew that if the pastors and their congregations would read *Glory* they would move into the revival quickly. I immediately sought out a person to translate *Glory* into Norwegian and a printer to print it, and the book is now available there. I believe that this same thing applies to nation after nation. I am desirous of having *Glory* published and distributed in all the nations of the world, as I believe it to be a powerful instrument of revival, and I trust that some of you who are reading these words will help to bring this to pass.

The people of Latvia translated the book, printed it and distributed it on their own. This revival will not only touch America "from sea to shining sea," but it will reach out to every nation. When we look at the vast numbers of people who need to be touched by this revival, we see that we need such a medium to carry the message.

All across the world, God is using *Glory* to cause barriers to come down in the lives of pastors and to bring their people into things that should be normal in the life of the Spirit but have not been taught. One Assembly of God pastor told me, "Sister Ruth, when

I was first given your book, I didn't understand a word of it, but now that I have been touched by revival, the understanding has come to me by revelation, and my life has been totally changed."

I first met my friend Eli Mizrachi many years ago in the Prime Minister's office in Jerusalem. He asked me why I was so interested in world leaders and in capital cities. I answered that this passion had been birthed in my spirit in the prayer meetings I attended as a child where the glory of God was present. Looking back on it now I recognize that I have a God-given heritage for the nations and for revival.

My grandmother Ward moved to Washington, D.C., when Mother was only six years old, and she is now eighty-seven, so that was more than eighty years ago. Grandmother searched for six months before she found others of her Pentecostal faith, but she finally found a little Pentecostal church down at the wharf on Water Street and joined herself to it.

The pastor of the church, Rev. Collier, was a very holy man, with a deep burden for the city and the nation, and he prayed for revival almost around the clock for two whole years. Grandmother met with one of the ladies of the church each morning, and they prayed for revival for Washington for several hours each day. God honored their prayers, bringing revival. After a time, the church had to move into much larger quarters. The attendance in Sunday school eventually reached fifteen hundred.

It was in that church at North Capital and K where
my father was saved and filled with the Spirit, and
where he would later become the Superintendent of
the Sunday School. He told me that many diplomats,
ambassadors and other dignitaries, both American
and foreign, attended the church where the pastor had
all nine gifts of the Spirit in operation.

As a young man Daddy worked for W.J. Sloan, a
well-known furniture company. Through this job, he
was in and out of the White House, the Capitol Building and other U.S. government buildings and foreign
embassies regularly. The greatness of those places and
the people who worked there rubbed off on him, and
he never forgot the importance of our nation's capital.

We never missed a presidential inauguration. The
20th of January was Daddy's birthday, and he always
said that the parade held in Washington on that day
every four years was in his honor, and even though
we lived in Richmond, we never missed it. Both of
our grandmothers were living in the capital city, so
we would go up early, spend some time with them,
and then go to the inauguration. Standing and watching each of our presidents sworn into office imparted
into my spirit a sense of patriotism, national identity
and destiny even as a girl.

Grandfather Ward was a Baptist evangelist who
traveled all over the world preaching when travel was
still fairly uncommon. He would come home with
pearls from Japan or silk from China. He had a won-

derful oratorical ability and could speak phrases in at least sixty-five languages. He also traveled and spoke extensively throughout America. For a time he was one of the lecturers for the famous Chautaqua Institute program. He memorized lengthy lectures that he gave all over the country, speaking for several hours a night in an attempt to uplift and encourage the American people. More of our family's heritage can be found in Mother's book, *God of Miracles.*

Personally, my focus was drawn to Washington and America after living many years overseas. I had come home to attend the Second Inauguration of President Ronald Reagan. During Reagan's first inauguration, I had gone with friends in political circles to some of the breakfasts held around the capital on the morning of the inauguration. During each inauguration, many such breakfasts are held, some by the party that has won the election, and others by various Washington power brokers. People who are considered to be of importance in the community are invited to attend. This is all fine, but where were all the praying people at a time like this?

I found that because Washington is very crowded on Inauguration Day, many people who have ministries there go out of the city for the day to avoid the hustle and bustle. Wouldn't it be wonderful, I thought, if someone would organize a prayer meeting for inauguration morning which all the ordinary people could attend. Should we not give special attention to this, the most important day on our nation's calendar?

These thoughts were strong in my spirit as I walked through the corridor of the Sheraton Hotel the morning of President Bush's inaugural. I was concerned that there was not a single prayer meeting we were aware of that we could attend on that very important day for America and the world. When I mentioned this to my friend, Connie Snapp DeBord, who was Director of Media in the Pat Robertson Campaign and later was a party unifier in the Bush Campaign Headquarters, God spoke to me and told me to organize such a prayer gathering. I told Connie what the Lord had said, and she answered, "You can do it, but you would have to make the arrangements at least a year in advance." I began planning for it for the next presidential inauguration.

When God spoke to me to host the Presidential Inaugural Prayer Breakfast four years later, we didn't know who would be the president-elect or which party would win the election. We didn't even know who the candidates would be. When Bill Clinton won the election, many Christians made it a point to boycott the inauguration that year and, instead, met in Philadelphia for prayer.

The well-known syndicated columnist and commentator Cal Thomas wrote an article which he was kind enough to fax to me before it appeared in the newspaper in which he said, "He asked for bread, and they give him a stone." Bill Clinton had spoken in his Baptist church before leaving for Washington and had asked Christians everywhere to pray for him. Instead, everyone was ready to stone him.

We knew that, whether or not we agreed with his every point of view, he was our president and we were called to support him with our prayers.

The Lord gave me the privilege of meeting Annette Lantos, the wife of Congressman Tom Lantos, in Jerusalem and, later, the congressman himself. We became good friends. They arranged for me to be the guest chaplain for the day in the U.S. Congress. On February 14, 1995, I stood before the representatives of the various states and led them in prayer. After I was introduced by the Speaker of the House, Newt Gingrich of Georgia, I prayed:

> *Holy are You, oh Lord, just and righteous in all Your ways. You are awaking and healing our nation by Your presence in this crucial hour, in this strategic day, for Your presence heals, creates and effects change, not only in our nation, but in all the nations of the world. We declare the hastening and fulfillment of Your plans and purposes for our great nation through these yielded men and women who have been given authority by You and the people of this country. Be unto us wisdom, knowledge and understanding, and establish peace, justice and righteousness*

in all our dealings. Let Your love be shared among
us.
Thine is the kingdom and the power and the glory,
and may Your glory fill these chambers.
Hallelujah!

> *In Your name I pray,*
> *Amen!*

I declared that the glory of the Lord would fill the chamber and fill our nation, not even realizing that I would be given the privilege of coming back to America to help to bring this to pass.

As I came down from the podium, the first person I was introduced to by Chaplain Ford was Congressman Bill Richardson from New Mexico. He was to become our Ambassador to the United Nations under the second Clinton administration, but as congressman he was already trouble-shooting for the president and had just come back from North Korea. When he learned that I was interested in going there, he said that he would help me. Because of the timing, it proved not to be easy, but he tried. Later, God used Pennsylvania State Senator Stewart Greenleaf, Jr. to accomplish it.

When we left the Chamber of the House of Representatives we were invited to the cafeteria of the Sam Rayburn Building for lunch. Many congressmen sat at tables all around us. I saw Mrs. Madeleine Albright, then our Ambassador to the United Nations and soon to be our first woman Secretary of State in the second Clinton administration. I hurried over to her and introduced myself, and we spoke for a few minutes. When God gets into the picture, He knows how to put us in the right places with the right people to get the assigned task accomplished. I have had further contact with her since then.

Exactly a year later, in February, I had the privilege of being the Guest Chaplain in the Pennsylvania State Senate for two days. After saying the opening prayer, I was permitted to remain in the chamber all day. I sat and prayed for the state and the nation. It was very meaningful to me to be able to return to the very womb of America and intercede for revival.

In April my brother was given the opportunity of being the Guest Chaplain of the Pennsylvania State Senate, as well.

God is elevating His people for the sake of revival. Believe for it, and He will cause it to come to pass.

If we can keep our eyes on the heavenlies, God is going to do the work for us. Let us see the eternal, the invisible things of God.

Because God is anointing us more and more to look into the unseen realm, look for the eternal in every service. Look for the glory. Look for the manifestation of it. Let God anoint you unto the excellence of this new day.

Be lifted up in the Spirit. Rise to the challenge of the hour. Be the man or woman that God needs to serve as the channel of His blessing in this revival hour.

Last year someone had a dream that my brother rode home in a buggy with the old-order Amish people. My brother died before this occurred, causing the dreamer to be disappointed. A few months ago God suddenly opened ministry among the old-order Amish for the Akers family who are part of our ministry in Ashland, Virginia. It began with them going to pray for the sick and they have continued to do special services of praise and worship. I encouraged Sister Akers to take my brother's book *Hear the Voice of God* and my book *Glory* as a gift to be given to them. When they got in their buggies to return home, Sister Akers suddenly got so happy, realizing that my brother was riding home in the buggy with them, as his picture is in the back of the book. Revival glory is beginning among them.

✳ *Lord,*

We decree, in the name of Jesus, for everyone who is reading these pages, an excellence of spirit beyond anything they have ever flowed in before. Lord, You're raising us up for Your eternal purposes. You're raising us up, Lord, in this day and hour for revival; and we will not falter, and we will not fail. We will not stumble. We will be lifted up into the realms that You have prepared for us for revival glory.

We lay aside the temporal and take on the eternal.

Praise your name, Lord.
Amen!

Chapter 3

Getting Ready for Revival

In the year that king Uzziah died I saw also the Lord sitting upon a throne, high and lifted up, and his train filled the temple. Above it stood the seraphims: each one had six wings; with twain he covered his face, and with twain he covered his feet, and with twain he did fly. And one cried unto another, and said, Holy, holy, holy, is the Lord *of hosts: the whole earth is full of his glory. And the posts of the door moved at the voice of him that cried, and the house was filled with smoke.* Isaiah 6:1-4

God is giving us the opportunity to get ready for revival. Many people feel that they cannot give Him the time needed for revival right now. Their lives are far too complicated, and their involvements are too many. God is dealing with us to set our affairs in order so that we will be available for that great and glorious move of God which is coming and, in many places, is already here.

A short time before the revival broke in the Brownsville Assembly of God Church in Pensacola,

Florida, God impressed my friend Marty Mitchell to tie up all the loose ends of his business and to retire and free himself for the Lord's service. He didn't understand what the Lord was saying. He thought he was just freeing himself to take an extended vacation and to do some other things he had been wanting to do for years. But soon after he obeyed the Lord and got his business affairs in order, revival broke, and he has been able to give himself completely to the revival in Brownsville ever since. Many other members of that great church had the same experience and were ready for revival when it came.

The Brownsville revival is impressive in many ways. I am especially impressed by the willingness of the whole congregation to rearrange their lives for revival. They include the choir members, the ushers, the ministry team, the administrative staff, the audio staff, the parking attendants, and others. Of course, my favorite member of the staff is Lils Terhune, the Chief Intercessor. They have all given themselves for the Body of Christ and revival.

At one of the pastor's conferences, Brenda Kilpatrick, Pastor John Kilpatrick's wife, and a minister in her own right, spoke on How to Survive Revival. She told about the many changes they had had to make in their own lifestyle. For instance, there was just no time to cook and bake the many delicacies they had enjoyed before. They had been forced to simplify their lives in every way.

It isn't that God is taking business away from His people. It is just that He is freeing His people to be able to flow together unto His goodness for the ingathering of the harvest.

During the summer of 1996 I was blessed to be interviewed in Jerusalem for a 700 Club telecast. The filming took place on Mt. Scopus overlooking Jerusalem. After the filming, I was able to speak with my friend Norm Mentil, the producer. He told me that he had been thinking a lot about what my brother had prophesied over him some months before. The Lord had said that He would remove the encumbrances from Norm's life. His question to me now was, "When will God do it?"

I smilingly replied, "Norm, sometimes God is waiting for us to help Him."

Later, in September of that year, my brother and I were again at the Revivalfest at CBN and saw Norm. He said that after the filming in Jerusalem, he had returned to his hotel room to relax. It had been a busy week of filming. He had read a chapter of *Glory* and then gone to take a shower. While he was in the shower, God had spoken to him about going on a forty-day fast. He was now at the end of that fast and looked absolutely wonderful. He had implemented the process that gets rid of the encumbrances, and he was ready for revival. I am hearing wonderful reports of how God is using him in praise and worship at the Presbyterian Church in Virginia Beach, Virginia, to bring people into the glory, as well as in other praise, worship and glory seminars.

A few years ago, the Lord spoke to us here at camp about setting our affairs in order. Some who heard His words found that it was not easy to put things in order, but we have to do whatever is required. When revival is in full flood, there will be no time. So don't wait; get ready now.

I tell people that if they haven't worn or used something in their closets or garages in the last two years, they should get rid of it. It was a sermon I preached along these lines that got my friend Bill Wilson of Atlanta, Georgia, moving. God had been speaking to him and his wife Connie about moving to Capitol Hill in Washington, D.C., to serve Him there. They were available to God because Bill had taken early retirement from his engineering position with the Georgia Department of Highways. They fully intended to move, but they were always hindered when they thought of the timing of moving by the thought of sifting through a lifetime of possessions stored in their basement. They would have to make decisions about what to eliminate and how to consolidate the rest for the move.

Bill was given a tape of that sermon, and he played and replayed it. As a consequence, he made many trips to charitable organizations, giving away the accumulations of the past, much of it treasured memorabilia, so that they could move. They made the move to Washington and have been on the moving chariot of revival glory ever since.

Time is not what it was in the past, and that doesn't seem to make sense. Days are still twenty-four hours long, and hours are still sixty minutes long, but in the Spirit there is a definite acceleration of time. Everything is moving faster.

What is happening around us is beyond comprehension, except when we get in the glory realm. When we are out of the glory, we may move by the rhythms of natural time, but when we are in the glory we experience that acceleration of the Spirit.

If time is moving so quickly, how can we get everything done? That's the mystery. In one sense there is an acceleration, while in another sense God is putting His touch of eternity upon what we do; and in eternity there is no limitation of time. So, when we stay in the glory there are enough minutes in every hour and enough hours in every day to get the job done, to bring in the entire harvest before Jesus comes.

I find that when God has a special task to be done, He finds a busy person to do it. Once, when my schedule was already totally full, I saw Him in vision putting a golden wedge into a clock, making enough time for me to do what He was calling me to do.

Not long ago, in one of our camp services, I saw a most unusual thing. God was dropping down moments from Heaven. It was the first time I had seen time in this way. We know that time is of the Earth and that we won't be bothered by the limitations of time in Heaven. Nevertheless I saw God measuring time and dropping it down to us. The most notable thing was that time was no longer counted to us in years or in months or in days. Every moment, I saw, is now precious and must count for God's glory. There's a shortness of time, and every moment is golden. Appreciate it, and use it to the fullest. Cherish the moments.

Last Wednesday night at our Richmond church, the whole service — the important songs, the prophetic, the preaching — was about the coming of the Lord. This was not prearranged. It was the spontaneity of the Spirit of the Lord. Sister Ruth Carneal, one of our ministers, told me of her vision of the service earlier that afternoon. She heard the audible voice of the Lord say, "I am coming soon." With the hearing of His voice, instantly everything was put in order in her life. Things suddenly lost their importance. He became life's priority anew.

In the days just ahead, we will see hundreds of thousands come to Christ in a single service. In the recent past, we rejoiced when it was known that twenty thousand new believers were being added to the Church in Africa each day, but what we are seeing now is surpassing anything we have seen before. That wheel within the wheel is moving ever faster. Normal times have passed, and we are now into a period of intense experience in God leading up to His coming. You may find it necessary to just take everything you have and throw it up to God. Let Him give you an abandonment of spirit. He will take anything you offer Him. He is accepting all your sacrifices.

The day for normal sermons has passed. God is doing unusual things. There must be a new urgency in our sermons, and the sermons themselves must be by revelation.

Some people need to throw their schedule to the wind and let God have His way with them. Throw your future up to God and let Him make of it what He will.

We must not return from the presence of God as we have come; we must return as different people. For the Lord is laying new anointings upon us. We must wear the glory upon our shoulders and be prepared to do whatever is necessary to get ready for revival.

There are some physical preparations to be made for revival. The facilities at our campground in Ashland, Virginia, are very basic. My brother was working toward getting additional buildings erected to house the growing crowds of people, but he had difficulty getting the approval of the County Planning Commission, so his plan was delayed.

Last spring, when I returned to Virginia from speaking at the pastor's conference in Brownsville, Florida,

I told him what I had seen there. The Brownsville church had no sleeping accommodations at all, yet people were coming from all over the world to attend the meetings and be blessed, and they were staying at local motels. Instead of concentrating on housing, the church at Brownsville was buying up neighboring houses, tearing them down and making parking lots. Parking space had proved such a serious problem for those coming from far and wide that some people were having to park miles away and walk back to the church before the church got additional parking.

In view of this, we decided to widen our entrance road and to upgrade and expand our parking facilities. My brother was in the process of doing this when the Lord took him home, but we were able to finish what he had started. If angels are going to call people to come to our services, we must get ready for those overflow crowds. God is giving us the visions, and God is giving us the fulfillment of the visions. We must do whatever is necessary to be ready.

Some doubt that revival can come to America. Some actually feel that God has passed America by, but they are very mistaken. God is moving across our nation, and the momentum of revival is growing quickly. Don't be satisfied just to see it. Determine to be part of it. I personally plan to be on the cutting edge of it. Some of you who are reading this will become key players in the revival and some of you will be used, not only in America but beyond America. The nations are ready for revival. Set your house in order, for God may want to use your life elsewhere as well.

If you want to be part of the greater things God is doing, you can be. If you want it, it will be yours. The Lord will lift you up and move you about and you will know that the hand of the Lord is mightily upon you and that all that has happened to you in the past has been to bring you to this day.

God is working on your behalf and has gone before you to prepare the way, so that He can do a glorious thing in you. He has set before you a broad gate. You will not have to squeeze through a narrow opening, for He has opened a broad door of entrance and acceptance for you, and you will be able to go in and accomplish all that He has called you to do.

I pity those who still believe that God is not speaking to His people today. God hasn't changed, and His desire to communicate with His people is just as real today as it has always been. He wants to speak to YOU. His voice will fall upon your spirit as ointment that brings healing to your spirit from every doubt and unbelief of the past. His voice will be a balm for every hurt and every wound so that you can walk forward in confidence and become part of the revival that is coming to God's people.

Get ready for revival!

Lord,

Fan the revival fires in me. Cause me and every circumstance of my life to be ready to be used in revival.

In Jesus' name we pray,
Amen!

Chapter 4

Declaring the Revival

The heavens declare the glory of God; and the firmament showeth his handiwork. Day unto day uttereth speech, and night unto night showeth knowledge. There is no speech nor language, where their voice is not heard. Their line is gone out through all the earth, and their words to the end of the world. In them hath he set a tabernacle for the sun. Psalm 19:1-4

There is a declaratory realm of the glory of God in which our voice can be heard *"to the end of the world."* We can stand in our own places and release our faith, reaching out to the isles of the sea, reaching out to the uttermost parts of the Earth, declaring the glory of the Lord, declaring revival for our day and for our generation.

God has not limited us, but we have limited ourselves by not fully believing in what He is willing to do through us. He is causing some greater things to be birthed in us, faith to believe for the harvest, faith to declare His purposes in all the Earth, faith to speak out for revival.

God has given to the Church a voice of declaration, and He is waiting for us to use it. He is quite ready to pour out His Spirit and His glory upon us in this hour, and if someone will just declare it, He will do it. This is not a declaration of your intellect; it is a declaration of heavenly intent; and when you declare something in the Spirit, God begins to put it into motion.

It is time to declare revival, for God has promised it. I believe that every Christian magazine should have a special section called "The Voice of Revival," where up-to-date news of what God is currently doing all over the world is presented. God will bless any magazine that does it.

Those who have regular radio programs need to do at least one segment a week about revival. Let us declare, by faith, what God is doing, so that He will do more.

God told me last year that any television station that would become a voice for revival would be kept solvent. Whatever media you may have, use it for revival. Declare revival for your nation.

One morning, as I was waking up in Jerusalem, the Lord told me that I should begin leading the people in singing *America the Beautiful* everywhere I go and that each time we sing it we should decree a blessing upon our nation. We have that authority, and it is time to use it.

The Lord wants us to become so consumed with revival that we can think of nothing but revival and

talk of nothing but revival. Let our lives be totally oriented toward revival. If you will do it, others will catch
the fever. This revival fever is catching, and if you
will get excited about it, others will too.

This is the hour of revival, and we must become
revival oriented. Speak it everywhere you go. Believe
for it every waking moment. Stand on the promise
of it.

I love that chorus *The River Is Here,* and I love to
wake up every morning and declare it. The river is
here. Revival is here. The glory of God is here. This is
the hour we have waited so long to see. This is the
moment we have all prayed for, and it's here.

Thank God it's in Toronto. Thank God it's in
Brownsville. Thank God for what He is doing in
Smithton, Missouri. Praise God for Wynnewood,
Pennsylvania, and Tampa, Florida. But I'm so glad I
can wake up every morning and declare, *We rejoice,
for the river is here.* It's here.

Stop dwelling on the negative and see what God is
doing. I feel sorry for those who are picking something out of the better-known revivals of our day to
criticize. Every single revival is of God, although each
may have its unique and peculiar aspects. The Toronto
blessing, the Pensacola revival, the Rodney Howard-
Browne revival, what God is doing in your local
church, what God is doing through the ministries of
Benny Hinn, T.D. Jakes, Oral and Richard Roberts,
Kenneth Hagin, Kenneth Copeland, Bonnie and

Mahesh Chavda, Monsignor Walsh, Gwen Shaw and many others like them, that new surge of the Spirit of God that is being felt literally all over the world — all these are of God. Our abilities to yield to what God is doing may be different and, therefore, the manifestations of God's power we experience may be different as well. But the more the revival progresses, the more we will find similarities rather than differences.

Stop trying to find fault with what God is doing and begin to declare blessing on your own people, your own family, your own town, your own ministry, your own soul. This is not a time to find fault or to place those whom God is using under a magnifying glass. Get your own blessing. Declare your own revival. The sooner you stop examining the things God is doing elsewhere and start decreeing a blessing upon your own town, the sooner you will see it come to pass.

God has said:

> *For the earth shall be filled with the knowledge of the glory of the* LORD, *as the waters cover the sea.*
>
> Habakkuk 2:14

Start believing for it and declaring it to come to pass. It's God's time. If the whole Earth is to be filled *"with the knowledge of the glory of the Lord,"* that means that *your* town and *your* house will be filled as well. Stop thinking it's impossible and start claiming it. God said it will happen. *! ! ! Yes, yes, yes !*

Too many times the things we know in the natural keep us from declaring the will of God for those around us. When I see a vision of the Spirit of God at work in our Capitol Building, I pay no attention to the ravings of the commentators who would make us think that all is lost in our political system. If God has shown me that He is working there, then I must believe it and declare it.

One day, in a vision, I saw God take the top off the Capitol Building. He picked up several men, as if they were chess pieces, and took them out of the building. Then He picked up several other men and put them into the building in their place. I believe it. I believe that God is in control of the affairs of men, and I must declare His will for our nation and the world. *"The Earth SHALL be filled with the knowledge of the glory of the Lord."* Why should I be afraid to declare it?

Let your voice speak forth with a great anointing and authority. Let it go forth to the ends of the Earth. When you make an effort to be included in the greater thing that God is doing, you cannot help but be enlarged personally. You lose nothing. Trust for the transforming graces of the Lord to be felt far and wide. What He is doing in the Earth is great.

When we first went to Jerusalem to live, the Lord told us to "see the good of Jerusalem." He reminded us of the experience of the twelve men who spied out

the land of Israel in Joshua's day. Ten gave a report
that God called *"evil."* Although what they said was
true, it caused a whole generation of Israelites to miss
out on the promises of God. The two men who of-
fered a good report were kept alive to lead the next
generation of Israelites into the Promised Land. God
told us that if we would see the good of Jerusalem
and only speak good about Jerusalem, He would keep
us in the land.

We had to cultivate this ability. I remember failing
one day. I nodded my head in agreement with someone who had made a negative comment about
Jerusalem, and I had to go to that person afterward
and apologize for doing that. God has helped us to
concentrate on the positive aspects of Jerusalem and
has kept us in the land as a result. This year we cel-
ebrated the twenty-fifth anniversary of our ministry
in the Holy City.

As we learned in Jerusalem, we have also acted in
America or wherever else we have been. Speaking
positively about a people, a city or a nation helps to
release your faith for that people, city or nation. Declare His glory wherever you are!

Refuse to have anything but optimism for the future, and refuse to speak anything but blessing to your
country. Stand together in unity and believe for God
to bless as He has promised. We are on the brink of
the greatest visitation of God the world has ever seen.
Determine to be part of it.

For several years now we have been singing a little song of declaration concerning the revival: *There's Going to Be Revival in the Land*. You can sing that one, or you can make up your own song and sing it. Let the very atmosphere be charged with your declaration of revival glory. I am believing for it, and I am determined to declare it by faith, as I watch it materialize by the power of the Spirit of the living God.

A sister from New England said to me, "Sister Ruth, I always felt bad when I would hear preachers talking about 'the frozen Northeast.' " The reason she felt bad, it turns out, was that God had given her a vision of a flame that was already burning in that part of the country. It wasn't a great flame, but it was a flame; and, by seeing it, she knew that not all the Northeast was "frozen."

She was so blessed when she attended our Presidential Inaugural Prayer Breakfast in Washington. When she heard me say that I saw flickering lights coming on all over the map of America, she realized that they were the same flickering flames she had seen coming in the Northeast, and she knew that God was going to send revival there.

When God has dropped into your spirit a vision for revival in America, you can no longer speak about this country in negative terms. You only see the fire burning. You only see more and more light coming. You only know that the winds that are blowing will eventually touch every area of America — north,

south, east, and west. And you know that this wind
of the Spirit will breathe new life into the dead and
cause them to stand upon their feet, *"an exceeding great
army."* It's already beginning to happen.

God is telling us that revival doesn't have to come
to each locale in the same way. You don't have to copy
what has been done somewhere else. This is a new
day, a new time and a new place. Let God do it the
way He wants to do it. But begin today to believe God
for revival in your area and to declare it openly and
boldly.

 Lord,

> *We want to see revival in our land more even
> than we want our necessary food. We declare re-
> vival glory from border to border and sea to
> shining sea.*

> > *In Jesus' name,
> > Amen!*

Chapter 5

Hungering for Revival

In the last day, that great day of the feast, Jesus stood and cried, saying, If any man thirst, let him come unto me, and drink. He that believeth on me, as the scripture hath said, out of his belly shall flow rivers of living water. John 7:37-38

God doesn't want us to be frustrated. If we hunger for His power and His glory, He will see to it that we are satisfied. The hungry will be fed. That's His promise. The thirsty will be satisfied. He never fails in this regard. If you are desirous of knowing, He will not leave you frustrated. He will cause you to know.

In one sense, the flow of the river of God in our lives is spontaneous, and we cannot control it. But in another very real sense, God does it in response to the hunger He sees in us. The river flows down from the throne of God, flows down into the very depths of our beings and flows out through us to others, and none of that is controlled by our own wills. The river has a will of its own. The Spirit is the river, and the river is the Spirit. The will of the river is the will of

the Holy Spirit. Therefore, we must join ourselves to
the purpose of the will of God.

But the prophetic word cannot come forth unless
you let it come forth. The other manifestations of the
waters of life cannot come forth unless you let them
come forth. Although the river has a will of its own,
you can prevent it from performing its desired func-
tion by not yielding. Let the river flow. *Yes, yes!*

I have seen the glory come in as a river and have
seen that it is not democratic. We can't vote on it. We
can't choose those to whom the river will flow. The
river has a will of its own. We can, however, have an
influence on the river. How is that? Jesus said it. *"If
any man is thirsty, let him come and drink."*

When you are thirsty, the course of the sermon will
change to accommodate your desire. God will move
the preacher from one flow to another so that all the
questions that are in your heart can be answered. Your
great thirst moves the heart of God like nothing else
can. You may try to influence God in a hundred other
ways, but nothing can do it like your spiritual desire.
He responds to your desire for Him.

The enemy of your souls knows the power of desire and would try to channel your thirst into any
range of other matters. Don't let him do it. Focus your
thirst. Direct it, and let nothing dilute the intensity of
it. Let your thirst for God grow and grow and grow
some more. Avoid things that might dilute it and
dwell on things that cause it to grow.

We must also work to create thirst in others. How do we do that? When people hear God speak, they want to hear Him speak more often. When they feel His touch, they want to feel His touch more often. Once they have experienced new revelation, they want to receive more new revelation. God knows how to make us hungry and He will do it for us — if we will let Him.

Many Americans are meat and potatoes people. They grew up on it, and that's what they enjoy eating. It's surprising how many don't like peas and carrots and other common foods. Tastes for many foods is acquired. I feel so blessed because of having lived and traveled in many other countries and having acquired a broad range of tastes for food. I can enjoy so many wonderful things the world over.

Sometimes when we have served special dishes in Jerusalem, for example, someone was heard to remark, "I can't stand asparagus." Well, it might be better not to develop a taste for it because it's very expensive. Each of us has a list of things we don't like. But when we do that, we are only limiting ourselves. We can enjoy eating many things that the ordinary person might not enjoy, or we can limit ourselves to the few things we acquired a taste for while growing up. The choice is ours to make. Nobody can force you to like something or to try it and see if you might develop a taste for it.

I want to declare that just as I have many acquired

tastes in the natural, I have many acquired tastes in the spiritual. When I was a small girl and felt the glory in certain meetings, I was spoiled by that, and I have never been satisfied with anything less. Very early in my life I acquired a taste for revival, and I have never been satisfied without it.

Many people who are hungry for God are frustrated by not having a church near them which is flowing in revival. It can be a problem, but it is no excuse not to get into what God is doing. It was my privilege to be involved with the Charismatic Renewal from the beginning, and most of the last forty years of my life have been spent in non-Pentecostal circles. I saw God reaching into every denomination. The only time I was with Pentecostal people was when I returned to the campground each year in Virginia.

Most of the people I worked with did not see their churches being thrown open to the move of the Spirit of God or their church leaders flowing with the river of God's glory. If they were truly hungry, however, they didn't give up. Those who meant business with God started some type of midweek prayer meeting in their homes or in some other convenient meeting place, and God prospered those meetings. One of our spiritual sons, Bette Mengistu, the apostle of the Ethiopian church, started such a meeting in his home in Nairobi, Kenya, and that meeting is now running about two thousand people each week. People are thirsty for God.

If your church is flowing in the river and the river is flowing in your church, count yourself blessed. Often, this is not the case. Some churches have a fine building, a lovely choir and marvelous programs, but there is no flow of glory in their midst and, therefore, little life. If that is the case with the church you attend, it is still no excuse for you to fail to get in the river and let the river flow in you. God responds to hungry hearts.

If you are attending a church where the flow of the river is not yet known, I encourage you to start a prayer meeting in your home where you can let God have His way. Make yourself available to God every day. The Lord will teach you, and you will know His hand on your shoulders in a new way in the days ahead. He will be so close, whispering in your ear, speaking into your heart, writing on your spirit. You can be among those who are simple, yet profound. You can know the mysteries hidden since the foundation of the world. You can know, not by the understanding of the flesh, but by the revelation of the Spirit. The Lord will lift you into His Spirit again and again until rivers flow in you and through you to bless all those around you.

People come to Israel from all over the world to attend various conferences, and I have noticed in the last several years that these people are ready for revival. The touch of revival that is being experienced in various parts of the world is creating a hunger, and people are willing to travel for the sake of revival. They want to be in revival meetings, and when they travel that far, their expectations are high.

Some of the local organizers of such conferences in Jerusalem have been very conservative people in the past, but they have been forced to open the conferences up more to the moving of the Holy Ghost because of the hunger of the people who were attending. The people were ready to move into the things of God, ready to rejoice, ready to dance, ready to pray more exuberantly and, because those who convened the conference wanted to be successful, they were forced to come into a liberty they didn't have before.

Revival is coming because of the hunger of the people. In former days, we often saw revival beginning on the platform and moving out to the congregation. Now, however, it seems to be beginning with the people themselves. This is forcing leaders to travel to places where revival is taking place and to get a touch of revival on their lives so that they will have something with which to feed their people. Some pastors, when faced with the changes that revival requires, are still reluctant. They sometime need several trips to revival sites before they are willing to throw everything to the wind and obey the voice of God. Traditions and inhibitions don't fall off easily. But if we are genuinely hungry for revival, we will do whatever it takes to achieve it.

If you desire it, anything is possible. Some people

who have never prophesied before, and certainly never over an individual, are prophesying as if they have done it their whole life. Once you get that freedom, it's yours. It may take some a very long time to make up their minds to stand on the end of the diving board and, longer still, to take that leap of faith. They may run up to the edge and back again several times, trying to get up their nerve. Once they have made up their minds to take the plunge, however, diving will become second nature to them.

You can ride a bicycle if you want, or you can stand back and imagine how very difficult it might be to do such a thing or how easily you could fall and hurt yourself. The choice is yours. You can drive a car, or you can think of all the reasons it would be too difficult and dangerous to learn. Many times our hunger or lack of hunger makes all the difference in this regard. If you are hungry enough for it, you will take the plunge and do whatever is necessary to learn. When you're not hungry, there is no motivation to even try.

When God says something to us, let us respond to Him immediately. Why should we wait? Don't wait for the end of the service. Don't wait for a better opportunity. Get so hungry that you go to the table the first time you are called.

If the water is there and the invitation is there and the opportunity is there, what are we waiting for? It is time to swim on out into the river of God.

I never was very good at doing the sidestroke. For some reason, I felt more comfortable looking straight ahead and moving forward, but recently in the Spirit I saw myself swimming with a sidestroke. The Lord is teaching us some new strokes and is strengthening us to be able to do them. He is giving us *"waters to swim in"*:

> *Afterward he measured a thousand and it was a river that I could not pass over: for the waters were risen, waters to swim in, a river that could not be passed over.*   Ezekiel 47:5

The water that God is calling us to swim in is wonderful, but unless we start swimming, we cannot know how wonderful it is. If there is no swimming, the water cannot be appreciated or utilized.

The waters of God are glorious. They are deep enough. They are pure enough. Start swimming. They become *"waters to swim in"* only if we get in and swim. Whether we are doing a new stroke or an old stroke, whether we are on our face or our back or our side, we are called to swim.

These are days for swimming. Don't even talk about the river unless you are ready to swim in it. If you try to get out into deep waters without being willing to swim in them, you might get yourself in trouble.

When the children of Israel came to the Red Sea, it looked to them like an impenetrable barrier. But no sooner had the Egyptians begun to approach them from behind than they got busy crying out to God for the sea to open. Sometimes God has to use the situations of our lives to motivate us to do the right thing. If you have no desire to swim on out in God's water, He may permit something to happen that will give you that desire.

This is not the time to harmonize and poeticize about the river. It is time to get in and start swimming. Some would describe the varying shades of color found in the river; some would speak of its fragrance; and some would concentrate on the fish to be found in it. None of that is wrong, but some people are so wrapped up in the river that they are known as "river people," but still they don't swim. Get in and start doing a few strokes. Stop picknicking on the banks of the river. Jump in.

To many people the things of God have become old, and they no longer have a sense of appreciation for them. Some of those who work in the Gospel are the worst offenders. If you talk about God, they think you have taken your work home with you. I enjoy being with those who talk about Him, those who never tire of hearing the same stories of His goodness over and over again. Unless you get hungry and cooperate with God, there isn't much He can do for you.

One of the changes we have made since our camp-meetings have continued on every weekend since the summer is to eliminate the afternoon service and push the lunch back an hour so that we can spend more time in God's presence. We don't want to be rushed when we are communing with God. We don't want to be rushed to get up from the floor if we happen to be lying there under the power of God.

We were so blessed as children because Mother and Daddy were so hungry for God. They were pastoring themselves, but any time they heard that God was doing something somewhere else, we would load up the car, stop on the way and get a loaf of bread, a small package of cheese, some bologna and a little mustard and mayonnaise to make sandwiches, and we would head off to the revival.

Imagine, as a child I had the opportunity to sit on the front row and hear all the great people who were flowing in God at the moment: Oral Roberts, William Branham, Jack Coe and many others. How blessed I was to have things sown into my spirit at that young age, things that have never left me, but have only continued to grow! In the anointing and in the glory, seeds of greatness are sown into our lives. It happens when we hunger.

When God is doing something, how can people be so blasé, as if they could not care less? That's not even polite. Let's get out and see what God is doing. Go, drink at the fountain and see how God is doing it. Each place He does it a little differently because our perceptions are different and our yieldings are dif-

ferent, but it's the same revival; it's the same river;
it's the same glory that God is pouring forth.

If we are thirsty, there is a simple solution. Come
and drink. The three elements are important. Be
thirsty; come to Jesus; and drink. When you do these
things, rivers of living water are guaranteed to flow
forth out of your innermost being.

We have no problem understanding these steps
when we are baptized in the Holy Spirit. Without a
hunger we will not come to Jesus. And once we are
there, we must take the step of drinking by faith, receiving what He offers us. And when we do it, a river
is released within us.

Let God birth within you today a genuine hunger
for revival, for He has promised:

> *Blessed are they which do hunger and thirst af-*
> *ter righteousness: for they shall be filled.*
>
> Matthew 5:6

Lord,

> *You have given us a hunger for Yourself and the*
> *manifestation of Yourself in all the Earth. We*
> *hunger for revival and revival glory. Satisfy us*
> *speedily, we pray.*
>
> *In Your name,*
> *Amen!*

Chapter 6

Prophesying the Revival

For we have not followed cunningly devised fables, when we made known unto you the power and coming of our Lord Jesus Christ, but were eyewitnesses of his majesty. For he received from God the Father honour and glory, when there came such a voice to him from the excellent glory, This is my beloved Son, in whom I am well pleased. And this voice which came from heaven we heard, when we were with him in the holy mount. We have also a more sure word of prophecy; whereunto ye do well that ye take heed, as unto a light that shineth in a dark place, until the day dawn, and the day star arise in your hearts: Knowing this first, that no prophecy of the scripture is of any private interpretation. For the prophecy came not in old time by the will of man: but holy men of God spake as they were moved by the Holy Ghost.   2 Peter 1:16-20*

There is a prophetic word at work in the world today that is beyond the control of man. It has nothing to do with what we have been taught. Those things that God has spoken into our lives cannot be controlled by the wishes of any other man. If we are willing to respond and move with the Holy Ghost, what God has spoken will come to pass, and no one alive can stop it.

The secret is our response when we are moved by the Holy Ghost. One of the most wonderful aspects of this current revival is that the Spirit of God is teaching us to respond to Him, and nothing could be more important. When God wants to speak, let us be those whom He can use.

Many people oppose prophecy because of some negative experience they had in the past, but is it any wonder the enemy fights us on the very thing that will be key to our elevation before great men? Those who have accepted the word of prophecy God is offering to His people today have experienced that this gift alone opens door after door to them.

There are times when God wants us to prophesy, and we would rather not, but Ezekiel prophesied as he was commanded. The place he was sent was the worst in the world, as far as he was concerned. He was a priest and, therefore, should not get near dead bodies. What harder place to have revival than a cemetery? It might not have been as bad if the bodies had been laid out in orderly graves, but as it was, the bones were just scattered around all over the place.

These bones were not just dry, they were *"exceedingly dry."* It's like saying that the people were not just dead, they were very dead and had been dead a very long time. I'm not sure why, but revival never seems to begin with those who are half alive. It usually starts where people are completely dead.

I remember when the outpouring of the Spirit came in California among the Episcopalians. Everybody thought that if revival began it would surely start with the Pentecostals, and if not them, then it would start with the Baptists. At least they were born again. But could revival begin with the Episcopalians? How could God visit them?

God usually begins that way, not with those who are half alive, but with those through whom He can show forth "the exceeding greatness of His power." He takes the most impossible of situations because He wants people to know that man has nothing to do with it. The will of man could maybe influence somebody that was half alive, but surely not those who are already dead. It takes the supernatural anointing, the power of God, the miraculous, for the dead to come back to life.

Every revival begins with the most unlikely people. The next one to get saved in your family may not be the one you expect to get saved. It will probably be the most unlikely candidate. Participate in it by prophesying the word of the Lord into your situation.

When the Bible was written it was because *"Holy men of God spake as they were moved by the Holy Ghost."* It didn't happen as a result of the will of man. You don't initiate it, you just respond to it. When you feel something churning within, when you feel something spinning inside, it is time to act.

When a prophetic word comes forth to us, that is a light shining into our hearts. It will pierce the darkness of our understanding.

We will not lean on our own understanding in the days to come. We will follow the prophetic word, that word that God has birthed in our spirits, no matter how impossible it seems.

This sure word of prophecy is coming unto us, and we, in turn, must begin to speak to others. There is a creative force that accompanies the prophetic word, and as you begin to prophesy, something begins to happen in the heavenlies.

If you don't have people to prophesy to, begin with mountains. Someone might say, "Are you kidding? Prophesy to mountains?" Oh, yes. Ezekiel was called to prophesy to the wind, and you can prophesy to mountains, to valleys, to cities, to walls, to whatever stands in your way. Say, "Oh, ye walls, come down, in the name of the Lord," and they will begin to topple.

Prophesy to fences. There are far too many fences still dividing brothers, and we need them removed. "Fences, come down, in the name of the Lord."

You may want to do your prophesying at first while everyone is singing or praying, so that you will not be worried who is hearing you. After a while, you will lose all such reserve and won't care whether someone is listening or not. At any moment, God may drop a word into your heart. Speak it out, and see what God will do. Holy men of old were moved by God, and men and women of today are still being moved by God to prophesy.

Prophecy sets in motion a creative force that no man alive can stop. Men can't control what is happening to you and to me. God is sovereign. When I say, "He is Lord," I don't mean that He is just Lord in my heart. He's Lord over my life. He is not only Lord within me, He is Lord round about me. He is the same Lord that said through the Psalmist David:

> *A thousand shall fall at thy side, and ten thousand at thy right hand; but it shall not come nigh thee.*   Psalm 91:7

This is not just referring to the conflict in Bosnia. God was talking about everything that the enemy would put in your pathway in an attempt to limit you. It won't come nigh you because you've made the Lord your habitation, and underneath His arms you are trusting.

Stop being distressed about people. Don't let your life be ruled by strivings with others. Don't allow divisions to be built up. Men might will the worst thing in the world for me, but every time they will something bad, something good happens to me. Therefore,

I refuse to look at the current circumstances and I look to the prophetic promise of God.

Prophecy is basically learning how to open our mouths and speak what God is giving us. We are moved by the Holy Ghost. Prophecy is His work, but He chooses to use our voices. He chooses to use our lips. He chooses to use our tongues. *Yes, Yes!*

We might prefer that He use someone else, but it is wrong to feel that way. We should be honored that God wants to use us.

Don't resist Him. The next time He knocks at your door and wants to use your lips, don't send Him away. Say, "Lord, I'm willing. I'm available. I want to be used of You. Move on me."

The men of old *"spake as they were moved by the Holy Ghost."* Their prophecy *"came not by the will of men."* The prophets of the Bible did not choose their post. Their gift came *"not by the will of man."* It came as they *"were moved by the Holy Ghost."*

Is it biblical for you to prophesy? Absolutely. The Bible declares: *"Ye may all prophesy"* (1 Corinthians 14:31). God won't force you to, but you may if you are willing. It's possible. It's permissible. If you are moved by the Spirit of the Living God, you may prophesy.

As Ezekiel prophesied something began to happen. I love that. That's the way it should happen. The results are not to be felt a year later. Something should start to happen even as we are speaking.

The Lord said to Ezekiel, "Prophesy again." It only takes two prophecies to bring revival. When you begin to be moved by the Holy Ghost, prophesy the first time and you will experience a shaking and a coming together. Then, you will be led to prophesy a second time. This time, you will not be prophesying to dry bones; you will be prophesying to the wind, to the very Spirit of God: *"Come ye, Spirit, and breathe upon these dead that they might live."*

When the Scriptures speak of the Spirit of God coming from the four winds, it means from the four corners, the four directions that the winds blow — the north, the south, the east, and the west. As the Spirit of God began to breathe upon those *"slain,"* they began to rise up as *"an exceeding great army."* This happened because *prophecy is the voice of revival. Let your prophetic voice bring forth the revival. You'll save yourself thousands of hours of vain activities* when you don't try to bring the revival in yourself. Speak it into existence by the power of the Spirit, and you will see men and women rise up to take their place as a great army.

Some people ask me what is more proper to say: "Thus saith the Lord" or, as many Charismatic people say, "So says the Lord"? It doesn't matter at all. You don't have to use the Old English. Use whatever language you are comfortable with.

Know that you are only the spokesperson, and expect that as soon as you say, "Thus saith the Lord," all Hell will perk up its ears and tremble. But don't worry; all of Heaven will bow its ears to rejoice with you and to bring to pass the prophetic word you have given.

Why do we even bother to say, "So says the Lord"? That's a very good question. We were taught, when we did spelling bees, to say the word, to spell it, and then to say it again. We were taught, when memorizing and reciting scripture, to say the reference (where the scripture is found), then quote the verse, then give the reference again. In this same way, it is good to start a prophecy with the words, "The Lord says to you," then give the message, and, afterward, conclude it with the words, "So says the Lord."

The other reason is that we don't want people to ever forget who is talking, the Lord.

The minute you open your mouth on the Lord's behalf, He begins to give you words to say. He is so pleased to have those who will speak for Him that He does not delay. If you doubt it, try it. There is no other way to become convinced. You may be amazed that God is using your voice and your lips, but you will know that He has raised you up and given you a sure word of prophecy that comes not by the will of man, but by the very movement of the Spirit of God.

What God wants to do in these last days can only be accomplished in the glory realm. We don't have enough time to do things as we used to do them. This is a whole new day, and we must stand and allow the prophetic word to do its work in the hearts of the people. Prophecy is powerful. Use it for the glory of God.

Are you holy enough for God to use you in this way? Well, how should we define holy? A holy person is one who is living unto God and letting God do the work. These were not perfect men, and you don't have to be perfect to begin prophesying either.

Ezekiel was carried away in the Spirit and told to prophesy. Paul was told, at the very beginning of his ministry, that he would prophesy unto many peoples. John the Revelator was told that he would prophesy to many people and many nations. Isn't it strange that we have the two apostles, one from the original twelve and the other *"chosen out of due season,"* both given the same message? They would prophesy to many nations and many peoples.

The nature of prophecy is unto many nations and many peoples. When you move into that prophetic flow, you have automatically multiplied your ministry to nations and to peoples and to kindreds. You may never prophesy in another language, but God can take that prophecy you give in English and cause it to affect nations. It will not be limited by the language in which it is given. There is no limitation in that prophetic flow.

God is raising up a prophetic voice to bless nations and kindreds and peoples, not by the will of man. We must join ourselves to the will of God, the purposes of God, the plan of God, and we will see revival coming forth by the Spirit in this day and hour.

You might say, "I don't know what to do." Well, that's okay. Just prophesy. Ezekiel said, *"So, I prophesied as I was commanded. And as I prophesied behold a shaking and a coming together."* You may see the scattered parts of what God is doing, all the various bones lying scattered about, but He wants to bring them together, bone to bone. You can prophesy into being the fullness of what God has planned and ordained for your life.

As you prophesy, believe for a shaking, and don't get too nervous when it comes. Take a deep breath, pause a moment, and watch what He is doing. The shaking often produces the coming together. Somethings have to get shaken loose so that they can come together.

God will shake the people, the places and the situations that He desires to bring together. And it will all come about as a result of that prophetic word. It's that simple. It's why the enemy fights the prophetic flow.

Those who have not yet read my brother's book, *The Power of Prophecy*, need to read it. In fact, read it two or three times. Let it get into the depth of your being. I find people preaching and teaching it all over the world now. It's powerful. It's good teaching, and it will bless you. Somebody told me that by the time they got to page seventeen they were ready to prophesy. Let your life be turned upside down as well.

Only people of vision can prophesy to the winds to

blow. Most other people could not care less. In their thinking, these bones are dead, they will always be dead, and there's nothing anyone can do about it. Since God says differently, we must release a prophetic word in every state that will bring forth revival across the land. His word will *"build and plant."* It might have to do some uprooting in order to get the building and planting started, but the end result will be building and planting:

> *See, I have this day set thee over the nations and over the kingdoms, to root out, and to pull down, and to destroy, and to throw down, to build, and to plant.* Jeremiah 1:10

It only took two prophetic words from Ezekiel to bring revival to a cemetery; two prophetic words were enough to turn scattered bones into a mighty army; and two prophetic words can bring revival to your town. It couldn't be more dead than Ezekiel's grave yard, for those bones had been dead for a very long time. God is moving in the most unlikely situations and doing the impossible. The prophetic word is creative and powerful.

In 1992, just before we had our first Presidential Inaugural Prayer Breakfast, I had gone to Washington, D.C., to minister to some of our people who had just moved there. That night as I was standing in their service, I had a very strange vision, and the Lord said to those present that night: "You want your voice to be heard in this city, and you have tried in many ways to make it heard, but the only way your voice will be heard is through the prophetic." The Lord promised them that if they would lift up their prophetic voices he would cause them to be heard, even in the bedroom of the president. As I prophesied, I saw the prophetic word going out of the pulpit and into the bedroom of the president; and when the prophetic voice went into the bedroom of the president, I saw it at work.

You might ask, "Sister Ruth, is prophecy that powerful?" It is. This is why you need to start prophesying in the midst of the congregation and let God bring forth his word. Let Him bring it forth into the board rooms of the Earth, into every situation where He desires to work. Let the prophetic voice, the creative flow, come forth.

I find that many times when I start to pray, I recognize that my time is very limited and I just start prophesying into being the things I feel in my spirit that God wants to do. It comes to a point where I'm not asking, I'm not knocking, I'm not seeking. I'm declaring. I have skipped over steps one, two, and three.

You might say, "But the Bible says, *'Ask and you shall receive. Seek and ye shall find. Knock and it shall be opened unto you.'* " Yes it does say that, but Jesus was teaching babes. God didn't tell Ezekiel to ask and seek and knock. He didn't tell John the Revelator to ask and seek and knock. There comes a time when you should just speak into being what God, by His Spirit, is laying on your heart. Prophesy to the dry bones; prophesy to the wind, oh, son of man.

Lord,

Anoint us with prophetic unction, that creative flow of the Spirit that You are releasing into the Earth in this day and hour. Help us to prophesy as You have commanded.

In Jesus' name,
Amen!

Chapter 7

Uniting for Revival

*Behold, how good and how pleasant it is for breth-
ren to dwell together in unity! It is like the
precious ointment upon the head, that ran down
upon the beard, even Aaron's beard: that went
down to the skirts of his garments; As the dew of
Hermon, and as the dew that descended upon the
mountains of Zion: for there the Lord commanded
the blessing, even life for evermore.*

Psalm 133:1-3

*And the glory which thou gavest me I have given
them; that they may be one, even as we are one:*

John 17:22

I have observed since the first day that God began
to teach us about entering into His glory that it is absolutely essential to have unity before one enters the
greater glory, but also that the greater glory brings
greater unity. It becomes a question of which comes
first, the chicken or the egg. There are moments when
I am sure that glory brings unity, and there are other

moments when I know that unity brings glory. They are part and parcel of each other.

God has ordained that we experience the oil of unity. If we are to have the glory of God, we must know the unity of the Spirit among brothers. The degree of the revelation of the glory will come in proportion to the way we allow God to unite us. This is precisely why the enemy fights unity and harmony in the Body of Christ. He knows that in the unity and in the harmony, the glory of God will be manifested, and the house will be *"filled with smoke,"* the manifestation of God's glory:

> *And the posts of the door moved at the voice of him that cried, and the house was filled with smoke. Then said I, Woe is me! for I am undone; because I am a man of unclean lips, and I dwell in the midst of a people of unclean lips: for mine eyes have seen the King, the* Lord *of hosts.*
>
>   Isaiah 6:4-5

It matters not what giftings, skills and abilities a person has if, in the midst of the giftings, skills and talents, there is only contention and strife, and no glory is revealed. God wants a house *"filled with smoke,"* a house full of His glory, and that comes as each of us says, with Isaiah: *"Woe is me!"*

So many times, when the glory is not present, we say, "Woe is he," "Woe is she," "Woe is the preacher,"

"Woe is the Sunday school teacher," "Woe is that other person." We seem capable of seeing only the faults and failures of others. But when the touch of God begins to come to us, when the glory begins to be manifested in our midst, suddenly we recognize that we are the *"undone"* ones. And it doesn't matter much if we are a little "undone" or if we are a lot "undone." Some people have conquered all the majors, but still have a lot of minors to deal with. Only the glory makes them aware of their lack and then corrects it.

Recently, I saw that if we want to have clarity of vision, there can be no mote or beam in our eyes which deflects the glory of God and His revelation. If a beam is present, it is because we have permitted it to be there. If a mote is there, it is because we have allowed it to be there. But God wants us to have clarity of vision. He wants us to see things with a clear eye.

I don't know about you, but I want to see beyond the moon and stars. I want to see into realms of glory. I want to see the face of the Lord in every service. I want to see those things which have been prepared for us from the foundation of the world. But it comes only as we can drop our petty infighting and unite in the Lord.

Just as the oil ran down from the top of Aaron's head down to his beard and on down his garments, to the very skirts, the anointing of glory will cover us completely in these last days as we join hands as brothers and sisters in Christ. It is impossible for us to sit together in heavenly places if we cannot sit together in the flesh, united by the Spirit.

When you purpose for unity, the enemy will throw everything he can in your direction, until you will despair of ever achieving it. We all believe in the admonition of the Scriptures:

> *If it be possible, as much as lieth in you, live peaceably with all men.* Romans 12:18

But the fulfilling of that admonition has not proven to be simple. It just seems to many of us that there is not enough lying in us. But God is accepting no excuses in these last days. It is unity or else. He is calling out a people to stand in the priestly office before the Lord who, from the top of their heads to the skirts of their garments, are anointed with the oil of unity. *How good and how pleasant!* I believe that the secret of unity is for each of us to focus our eyes more and more upon Jesus.

I can remember clearly some of my moments of greatest exasperation and frustration with people, but I can truthfully say that those moments are becoming less and less. The Spirit of God is faithful. He wants us to excel. He wants us to live in the cloud. He wants our houses to be continually *"filled with smoke."* In fact, He wants our houses to be known more for the continual presence of the smoke than for anything else that people might remember us for. Let people feel the smoke of God's presence when they visit you, and they will be moved by it.

We stopped asking people a long time ago what denomination they belonged to. It doesn't matter. It has nothing to do with revival. I don't care what denomination they belong to, and I am convinced that God doesn't care either. It is immaterial. God is bringing forth a holy anointing oil that causes brothers to sit together in heavenly places and not to feel the frustrations of one another's limitations.

Some people get so agitated just being in the same room together. How can we get God's oil flowing in our lives, if this is our attitude? When the oil of unity is present, it is easy for the house to be *"filled with smoke."* When the unity is absent, you experience a struggle. God cannot allow His glory to rest in that place.

When unity exists, you find things happening easily and quickly. The smoke becomes so strong it is almost like a curtain in front of you, like a thick fog that keeps you from seeing the car in front of you. More and more God is going to bring forth the glory of His presence in our midst. If you covet the smoke, you must also covet the oil, for the two go together — unity and glory.

When the brothers of Joseph came to Egypt, he told them not to return without Benjamin. I think that was because they didn't particularly like Benjamin, just as they had not liked Joseph. But if they were to benefit from the grain stores of Egypt and to avoid the terrible effects of the famine, they could not return without their brother.

Imagine! After all the years that had gone by, these men still had bad feelings against their brother. Unless you let God deliver you from your feelings against your brothers, you will still be struggling with them years later, and this will keep you from receiving God's best for your life. I have seen people robbed of great anointings and great ministries because they refused to deal with their bitter feelings against Joseph and Benjamin, both major players in God's plan for all of their lives.

Unless you bring with you your Benjamin, you will not have food in the time of famine. Dealing with Benjamin became the difference between life and death for an entire generation. Stop trying to ignore your Benjamins. Deal with them. You can't afford to ignore them if you want the glory of God in your life.

Sometimes, when we are experiencing great glory, God reminds me of people that I need to bless in some way. And, although I carry no grudges against those who have done us harm through the years, sometimes I haven't blessed them like I should. It is always easier to bless those who have shown us kindness. When I am in the glory, God shows me a list of those to be blessed. On the list are some that I consider to be "good" and some that I consider to be "bad," but He doesn't seem to make that distinction. The amazing thing is that when I am in the glory I don't make any distinction either and am able to go down the line, blessing each one, whether they seem to me to be "good" or "bad." I cannot afford to harbor ill will against my brother and miss what God is doing in my own life.

How good it is! How pleasant it is for brothers to dwell together in unity!

Unity brings a pleasure many of us have not known until now, unity with those who have opposed us, unity with those who have maligned us, unity with those who have done us wrong. Only God can do that for us. Only He can cause us to *"sit together in heavenly places."* Those who want the glory will deal with their Josephs and their Benjamins. Those who want the glory will allow the Spirit to bring forth the miracle of forgiveness within them so that they can be *"one."*

Some would say, "That's fine. I can make peace with everyone except ... ," but there are no exceptions in this regard. Forget the exceptions. Forget the excuses. It is the very person you want to make the exception that God is calling you to reach out to and embrace in His love.

The enemy makes sure you hear all the bad things people say about you just before you bump into them on the street. I have experienced it many times. As I saw that person coming down the street, I had to say, "Jesus, help me," and He did. The enemy is dedicated to disunity, but God is dedicated to healing divisions among brothers.

God's honey buckets of anointing are waiting just above our heads. He is ready to pour out His glory upon us — if we will properly deal with whatever it is that is hindering us.

I find that when I cry out for His help, God is there and always answers, and when I do meet a person who has wronged me, I can genuinely embrace that person with Christian love. I know that's not "normal," but God knows how to perform the miracle.

Look the person right in the eye; reach out and take his hand; embrace him in God's love; say to him, "God bless you, my brother"; and mean it when you say it. Say it with faith and with sincerity, believing that the blessing of God is going forth into his or her spirit. You can do it because the supernatural strength of the Lord is available to you.

If you want to be those who know the house *"filled with smoke,"* be those who experience the flowing of the oil of unity. It doesn't matter if you don't agree totally on doctrinal issues. Enjoy the praises of God together. And when you are all focused on the goodness of the Lord, at that moment there is unity. It is He that unites us, not our doctrinal positions.

I have been enjoying moving in Charismatic circles for so many years that I thought I had totally overcome the obstacle of labels. Then one day in Jerusalem I found myself distressed because one of our people had become close friends with someone I felt did not have good doctrine. When I recognized what had happened in my thinking I had to make it a matter of prayer. I said, "Lord, I am determined not to let this difference of opinion bother me. Help me in this matter." And I never thought about it again.

Some of the points we argue about endlessly just don't matter, in the light of eternity. Get a taste of eternity, and you will forget about a lot of your doctrinal hang-ups. Say, "Woe is me," and let the Lord take out of you anything that hinders, any disunity, any lack of appreciation of others. Don't let your own lack hinder your progress in the Spirit.

Some of you might say, "If you had a husband like mine, you wouldn't say that we should make peace with everyone." But God has enough love for that husband of yours and ten others like him.

I was in Philadelphia some time ago and a friend took me into a Chinese restaurant belonging to Mary Ho. It had been a popular restaurant for years, but people who went there endured the fighting between Mary and her husband, only because the food was so good. Then, about a year before I met her, Mary had come to know the Lord. She told me, "After I knew Jesus, I looked at my husband with brand new eyes. We had been married thirty years, but suddenly I had an overwhelming love for him."

The fact that Mary Ho and her husband are not fighting anymore was immediately apparent to all the clientele of the restaurant, and that spoke louder to them than many words could have, concerning the power of God to change a life. God has enough love to go around.

Once, when some people in Jerusalem had wronged us, God spoke to me and said, "It's not enough for you to forgive them. I want your heart to be so changed that if they should stand before you, you could prophesy into their lives every great thing you want me to do for you." I wanted that ability and, thank God, He has given it to me. We may have some lapses from time to time, but those times are becoming more and more rare as we remain in the glory. We are determined to strive for the unity of the brethren.

It is possible to be singing the same song and dancing the same dance and not be in unity, so let the oil of God's anointing come upon you to make you one with your brothers.

I feel that this subject is so important. Those who wish to know more will find a further discussion of this subject of unity in my book *Glory*.

Our Heavenly Father,

Pour in that precious anointing oil that causes brothers to sit together in unity. Let our houses be filled with the smoke of the glory of God.

In Jesus' name we pray,
Amen!

Chapter 8

What to Expect from Revival

Come, and let us return unto the LORD: for he hath torn, and he will heal us; he hath smitten, and he will bind us up. After two days will he revive us: in the third day he will raise us up, and we shall live in his sight. Then shall we know, if we follow on to know the LORD: his going forth is prepared as the morning; and he shall come unto us as the rain, as the latter and former rain unto the earth. Hosea 6:1-3

I have met many people who are revival specialists. They can tell you the details of every revival that ever took place and why and how it happened. They have read every book available on revival. But many of those people miss revival when it comes. In fact, some of them wouldn't know a revival if it shook hands with them. There are rare exceptions, and Steve Hill of the Brownsville revival seems to be one of them.

In every revival, there are certain things that we should expect. For one, we should expect souls to be saved. A good example is the great salvation revival that is taking place at the Brownsville church in Pensacola, Florida. I'm not sure of the exact figure at the moment, but probably several hundred thousand have been saved in that revival over the past two and a half years.

Certainly Steve Hill has one of the greatest abilities for giving altar calls of anybody I know. He is tenacious when it comes to winning souls. He just won't let go until people respond. I have seen him leave the platform and go into the balcony and into other sections of the church, looking visitors right in the eye and asking them point blank, "Are you ready to meet the Lord tonight? If you're not, come on down to the altar."

Steve was a street preacher and a missionary in the Argentine revival and has an uncanny ability to reach out to sinners. His altar calls are wonderful, and he is great at teaching others how to give good altar calls as well. Too many preachers, when they give an altar call and the people don't respond immediately, move on to the next thing and let it go at that. Steve just won't do it, and he has been greatly rewarded for his tenacity of spirit.

Every revival should also experience the healing power of God. Although the Pensacola revival began largely as a salvation revival, I was glad to see it move into this area, as well. Healing is a powerful tool for evangelism. When people are sick, they are looking for ways to get well, and the healing power of God can bring them to the feet of Jesus.

Healing doesn't have to dominate our services. We can take a few minutes of each service to minister to the physical needs of the people. It can be done through the word of knowledge, by speaking out the needs God shows you in specific people and declaring their healing. You can do this without calling people to come forward, and many can be healed in a short space of time. Healing doesn't have to be the whole service, but in great revival, healing should at least be part of it.

In times of revival, we can expect the Lord to set for us His banqueting table. The House of the Lord becomes the banqueting house, and there we are served more than daily fare. We may be accustomed to eating meat and potatoes or another vegetable and a salad, but at a banquet, there are many varied items from which to choose. You would never eat a whole meal of any one of them, but, rather, you want to have a taste of many, a variety of good things to eat. Revival brings us that variety. It brings prophecies, miracles, the baptism in the Holy Ghost, deliverance, release from emotional problems, laying hold of the promises of God concerning finances, and a wide spectrum of other blessings that God is pouring out in the Earth. In the midst of the glory, some will be called to preach — whether at home or out among the nations. All of this should happen in revival glory.

Prophecy should be a part of any revival. I so admire Lindell Cooley, the man God is using in Brownsville to lead the revival music. People who find themselves in a similar position must recognize that when they lead the people to the top of the mountain in praise and worship, God always speaks at the top of the mountain. For those who cannot yet hear His voice, there should be a prophetic voice raised up to address them. Since those who lead the worship are at the keyboard or microphone, they can very easily flow in the prophetic word. Lindell has been doing that very beautifully in the Brownsville revival.

There is a broadness to the purposes of God in every service. Let us look for more than one aspect of the Spirit at work in our midst.

Revival is a time for miracles and God is telling us that we are moving into the day of creative miracles and that we should all believe Him for it. My friend Jimmy Smith prayed for a girl who was born as a Thalidomide baby in Ireland. Those who were affected by that widely-prescribed drug were often born with partially formed limbs. This young lady had one small hand that seemed to dangle from her shoulder, and all her life she had only one desire, to someday be able to reach down and touch her waist.

He laid hands on her in the service, she fell out under the power, and her arm began to jerk. As her arm jerked, it began to extend further and further until, by the time she got up off the floor, her arm was a normal length, and she was able to touch her waist for the first time in her life. Needless to say, she was thrilled.

That's the type of miracle God wants to do more of in these days, creative miracles with the eyes, creative miracles with face structure and with parts of the body that have been missing or deformed, either through birth defects or accidents. Benny Hinn tells me that he is experiencing this type of miracle in his meetings. When I was with him in Miami recently, he said that it was the greatest meeting of his life, but two weeks later, when he was in Nashville, that meeting superceded the Miami meeting. This is all part of the tremendous increase that God is bringing in miracles in our midst.

I want to repeat something I mentioned in my book *Glory:* Once, when I had just returned to Jerusalem from an overseas trip, I walked into our fellowship, and I felt the glory of God as I had never felt it before. It was absolutely awesome! I suddenly knew how easy it is to raise the dead and to heal all manner of sickness and disease. How easy it is in that realm of glory! How easy to see people leaping out of wheelchairs and off of stretchers! How easy to see blind eyes opened and deaf ears unstopped! In that glory realm, nothing is impossible.

That glory stayed with us for several hours, as God was giving us a foretaste, as He often does, of a greater day, so that we could encourage ourselves and others to move into the glory realm.

When the fifth edition of *Glory* was being readied for press, I added a postscript, and, since those who bought the earlier editions may not have it, I want to also repeat something I said there: One night in Jerusalem I was carried away in the Spirit and saw a large platform. It was the deepest platform I had ever seen. I have stood on very broad platforms, but never on one so deep. On the platform there were at least a hundred hospital stretchers filled with critically ill people. I knew that they were there because of the miracles that were taking place in the meetings. I saw television cameras and reporters from all the major networks and knew that they were recording the great revival. I saw America ablaze with God, and I knew that when the revival had fully been ignited across America, Dallas, Texas, would be the center of it. It's coming, just as I saw it that night.

Each revival seems to be known for a different word. In the Toronto revival, as those who ministered laid hands on the heads of people, they said, "More!" They were encouraging the people to seek *more* and letting God know that they wanted *more*. In other places, those who minister have been known to say, "Now." They mean for the Lord to do the work *now*, and for the people to open themselves and receive from Him *now*. In other places, those who minister have been known to say, "Fire!" They are believing for the fire of the Holy Spirit to fall upon the people. Another common revival word is "Fill." We want God to fill us with more of Himself. Benny Hinn stretches out his hands in the direction of the people and says, "Touch!" He is believing God to touch them by His Spirit.

More! Fire! Now! Fill! Touch! It doesn't matter what word you use, as long as people receive the glory that God is longing to bring forth in this day and hour.

Be open to any other unique miracles that God wants to do. Many people are not.

Mother and Daddy took us to all the revivals that were happening in our childhood, and in the process taught us to keep an open mind to new things and to have an appreciation for the ministry of others. They taught us to be very careful not to grieve the Holy Spirit, and part of that teaching was to be careful what we said. People are much too quick to criticize what they don't understand and haven't personally witnessed before.

Before we were able to attend the meetings of Brother A.A. Allen for ourselves, we had heard people talking about the strange phenomenon being experienced in his meetings of oil appearing on people's hands and even flowing from their hands. I was in my teens by then and overheard preachers that I respected making fun of this phenomenon. They said, "It's nothing more than perspiration. They just rub their hands together and make them sweat. This is nothing more than a show. Everybody wants to get up front and be seen, and they will do anything to call attention to themselves."

Our parents never joined in these accusations. They were wise enough to withhold judgement until they could see for themselves what was happening. They knew the Holy Spirit, and they were sure they would know something that was real from something that was false; so, until they had seen it for themselves, they would offer no opinion. I never heard either of my parents say anything critical about what someone else was experiencing in God. They were so hungry for God themselves that it made them open to new things. They didn't want to do anything that would hinder the move of God's Spirit.

We traveled from Richmond to Pittsburgh to be in the Allen meetings, and when we got to the tent, we found it to be packed with thousands of people. One of the first people who drew our attention was one of the ushers who was leaning against a tent pole very near the back. He was leaning in such a way that his hands were behind him. They were resting on his hips, but he had his palms upward so that the oil that was coming from them would not drip onto his pants. He was not creating any sort of show. He was not waving his hands or showing them to anyone. To the contrary, he was just leaning against the pole, weeping and expressing his love to Jesus. When I saw this, my heart was totally melted. I realized that I had allowed the criticism I heard from others to get into my heart and affect my feelings about the oil on people's hands — even before I had personally witnessed it. Once I had seen it, I knew that it was of God.

One night near the end of our Summer Campmeeting this year, a young woman, who, along with her husband, had been a missionary with Wycliff, came to the meetings. I had never seen her before. After she had been in the meetings for several days, she came up to me to say that she would be leaving the next day and that she wanted me to pray for her. As I was praying for her, I looked down and saw that her hands were filled with oil. When we had finished praying, I pointed to her hands and asked her, "Have you ever experienced this before?"

She looked at her hands with astonishment and said, "Never!"

It was late and there were only a dozen or so people left in the Tabernacle. I said to those remaining, "This sister has oil on her hands. I want her to come and show it to you." She walked the five or six steps to the edge of the platform, and when she got there, she showed her hands to the others. They all wanted to be touched by her hands, but when she reached out her hands to them, some of them were so hungry that they sort of wiped all the oil out of her hands onto their own. When I saw it, I said, "Oh, don't wipe it all off. I want Brother Dwight Jones to see this." (He was the one who had ministered that night, and he was in the snack bar.) She started walking back toward me, and by the time she had walked those five or six steps back from the edge of the platform to where I was seated, her hand had again filled with oil. I encouraged her to go to the snack bar and show Brother Jones the supernatural manifestation of oil that was flowing from her hands.

I have experienced oil on my hands many times, and this is one of the reasons I don't use other types of oil to anoint the sick. When the Lord has given us supernatural oil, what else can compare? Many times, when I am preaching, oil drips from my face. Some would argue that it is perspiration, but it's much more than that. When I was with Monsignor Walsh at the Presentation Cathedral in Wynnewood, Pennsylvania, in September of this year, I ministered three nights. On one of those nights, the priests commented about the oil they saw dripping from my face as I was ministering. God is giving us wonderful signs and wonders to confirm His Word.

> *Behold, I and the children whom the LORD hath given me are for signs and for wonders in Israel from the LORD of hosts, which dwelleth in mount Zion.*   Isaiah 8:18

Stay open to God and what He is doing. It may seem strange to you at first, but eventually you will understand it. A pastor from St. Louis, Missouri, read my book *Glory* and decided to make a trip with his whole family to the Summer Campmeeting. When he got there, however, he found the meetings to be so free that he was offended and wanted to leave immediately. The family sat up late into the night trying to decide what to do. Should they go to some beach and try to redeem some of their vacation time? They finally came to the conclusion that they had spent so much to come to the campmeeting and had set aside the week just for that purpose, so they might as well stay and try to enjoy it.

Little by little, their opposition to the free style of worship began to fall away, and after some days the pastor said to me, "After we read your book *Glory*, we tried to implement some of it in our church. We didn't get nearly as free as you folks are here. In fact, we only got as far as wiggling our toes inside of our shoes."

But that was a great advancement, so I said, "Oh, that's wonderful. Keep wiggling, and more liberty will come." It was just a few nights later that I looked back during the course of the service and saw that his arms were beginning to wave and his whole body was swaying before the Lord. I was so blessed!

God is working on all of us. Pastor Benny Hinn has always been outrageously flamboyant himself, but has wanted the people who attended his meetings to be rather conservative. One night during Benny's meeting in Miami, he looked back in the arena, where some twenty thousand people were standing (and four or five thousand were standing outside, unable to get in), and he saw a group of young people who were flowing with a wave motion, back and forth to the music. In the past, that might have bothered him, but he stopped everybody and, pointing to the group of young people, said, "Look at those young people. They are waving to the Lord. Let's all do that." And suddenly he was leading more than twenty thousand people in a great wave movement before the Lord.

Revival is changing all of us, and we are getting more liberty. Later in the service, he turned to someone who was dancing and said, "Go ahead and dance!" God is freeing us all to praise and worship Him with all that is within us.

Another of the important signs or wonders He is giving us these days is falling out under the power of God. When people cannot control themselves and helplessly fall down in the power of the Spirit, it encourages them to know that God is real and that what He is doing in them is also real.

One of the greatest signs of every revival is the new music that God brings forth. When I first went to Brownsville, I noticed that they were still singing Vineyard songs and songs from Toronto, and I mentioned to Lindell Cooley that he needed to believe God for original songs of the Spirit. The gifting of music that comes forth with new songs is a sign that revival is in full swing. He had such a wonderful repertoire of everybody else's songs that it must have seemed unnecessary, but he soon began to reach in and allow God to give him new songs. Now, in most every service in Brownsville, you can hear a song or two that is being given spontaneously at the moment by the Spirit of God. Every great revival produces its own music.

Not everything about revival is pleasant. Every revival is persecuted, and often that persecution comes from those who were involved in the previous revival. They think God has to do things in the same way He did it with them, and if it is done differently, they imagine that it cannot be from God. When I heard, recently, that persecution was coming to the Brownsville revival, I was reminded of God's command to the children of Israel as they marched around the walls of Jericho. They were told to hold their peace for six whole days, and God would give them victory. That is often the most difficult thing for us to do, to hold our peace. It is so much easier to defend yourself than it is to be silent and let God defend you. If we can just remain silent long enough, the time for shouting will come, and the victory will be ours.

We should expect revival to sweep into many different denominational groups. I was speaking in a Baptist church one night when I saw the revival coming to the Baptists. It was coming in the back door. It was, I suppose, actually the front door, since we usually place our entrances at the back of the sanctuary. But whatever you want to call the main entrance, I saw a river coming through it and sweeping over the congregation.

The flow began with the people, before it swept to the platform and encompassed the ministry. God showed me that the river will get so deep it will be over the heads of the people seated in the pews of the Baptist congregations. The river must touch our heads, overcoming our reasoning minds, so that the Spirit can flow. Then I knew that we are about to see a move like the one we saw in the seventies that has come to be called the Charismatic Renewal. God will touch every denomination afresh, and this time, more people will participate in the revival glory and will stay in it.

We should expect the Holy City, Jerusalem, to be a very important part of the revival, and just as people are making the effort to travel to Pensacola, to Toronto, and now to Hendersonville (for the TBN Breakthrough Revival Explosion), we will see more and more people making their way to Jerusalem as well. God took us to live in Jerusalem so that we could sense the greater glory that is coming forth in that city. Of all the people we have known living there, our ministry has had a unique opportunity to know Jerusalem from the standpoint of the glory. For many years, we have had the opportunity to stand in the glory in the city through our daily prayer ministry.

There is no place in the world where the heavens are more open above a city than in Jerusalem, and those who go there are able to experience the revelatory realm in a far greater sense than they have known anywhere else in the world. In Jerusalem, God's glory is revealed.

When you go to Jerusalem, you must guard against being caught up in the historical aspects of the city only and even of knowing only where all of the biblical events took place. If God is taking us to the physical Jerusalem it is also to give us a greater revelation of the spiritual Jerusalem, the new Jerusalem that is coming down from God out of Heaven. God takes us to Jerusalem because He wants us to be a part of His last day purposes for the city and for the people.

Last Wednesday night God spoke in our service in Richmond. He reminded me that although I'm not living full-time in Jerusalem just now, I would always have a home and a ministry in Jerusalem. He said that there were two great doors in Jerusalem that He would yet open for me. This year our ministry in Israel has prospered under the able ministry of many anointed ones. Sister Nancy Bergen will be leading the ministry in my absence.

The glory of God will be manifested uniquely in Jerusalem in the days ahead and, because of that manifestation, a unique relationship will be forged between the Holy City and the rest of the world. Those who are interested in knowing further what God has in mind for the future of the city and its people can read my book, *Jerusalem, Zion, Israel and the Nations*. In particular, the book lays out God's purposes concerning Jerusalem and the other nations of the world.

Everything that God is doing is connected to what He is doing in Jerusalem. This year is the Jubilee year for Jerusalem and, in May of 1998, the country will be celebrating the fiftieth anniversary of the founding of the nation of Israel. This will also be a very significant year for the Body of Christ and for restoration in every area of our lives.

Loving the land of Israel and the people of Israel is not an option that God is offering to the Church. This is His heart. So, if you want to be part of revival, get caught up with what God is doing there.

One of the ladies who is being used in this particular area is Carol Howells, a niece, by marriage, to Reece Howells, the famous Welsh intercessor. I prophesied over her down at Pensacola, and she suddenly came to the forefront. God is doing unbelievable things through her.

Another thing we should expect in revival is to see an increase of angelic visitation. It's not that angels are suddenly active around us. It's that we have become more sensitive to their presence, more open to the revelation that makes them known to us.

The presence of angels became customary for the prophet Zechariah, as customary as the daily mail delivery or the coming of the newspaper boy. All aspects of the supernatural will increase in our lives until they become as real as the natural things.

Revival sweeps beyond national borders. In February of 1997, during our Winter Campmeeting, we had a visiting couple who were missionaries to Russia. As I was speaking, I looked back in their direction, and I saw the new Jerusalem just over their heads. I saw Moscow, and the New Jerusalem was hovering just above Moscow.

At first, I was quite amazed by the vision. I had no problem telling the brother about seeing the New Jerusalem, but that I was seeing it above Moscow seemed very strange. Only later did I realize that if Moscow is geographically directly north of Jerusalem, the heavenly city coming down over Jerusalem would, of course, overshadow Moscow as well.

As I looked into this vision of the New Jerusalem suspended over Moscow, the glory that I was witnessing began to come into my eyes and into my spirit, and I became drunk in my spirit from the glory I was witnessing. I saw that Moscow will have great revival, such great revival that as people in the past have gone to Moscow to be a blessing, they will go there in the future from many parts of the world to receive a blessing, drawn by the glory that will be manifested there. For days after I had the vision, I remained in the glory I experienced that night. The glory was so bright that I had difficulty keeping my eyes open in any service.

When the service finished that first night, the brother came to me and told me that before he had returned to America, he had escorted his wife out one day to do a business errand, and he sat in the car while she went inside a building to take care of the matter.

While he sat there, two angels came and sat with him and spoke to him about the revival that was soon coming to Russia. When his wife returned, he was unable to speak and could not tell her what had transpired. They didn't speak a word all the way home.

Later that evening, when the glory had dissipated sufficiently that he could speak, the man told his wife what had happened to him. She, too, had sensed something great and told him that when she had come back to the car, she had felt a sense of Heaven there.

All the Earth shall be filled with the knowledge of the glory of the Lord, including Moscow.

Our friends, Father Owen Lally and Sister Yvonne Zeller, spent thirty days this past summer in the glory. Father Lally is well qualified in the area of revival as he was actively involved in the Philippine revival in the early seventies when countless numbers of priests, nuns and laity were baptized in the Holy Ghost. The two of them published an appreciation of the several present-day revivals they visited and have sent their study out to Catholic leaders and laity across America. The following is what they have written about us:

> *Ashland, Virginia, was the sweetest expression of Revival that we saw. This community dates back to the great Revival at Azusa Street at the turn of the century. The Heflin and Ward families have been pioneers in Revival and their followers have evolved into a beautiful worship-*

ping people. The music was gentle and calm though lively and filled with joy. Dancing in the Spirit was a strong feature of their gatherings. Ruth Heflin is now the leader of the Community and her book entitled Glory *is truly a mystical gem. She has discovered the three archetypal steps into the experience of God's manifest presence. She herself is a very edifying witness to the beauty and importance of the Revival. She has a great love for the Catholic Church it seems and is most eager to help us in the birthing of the Revival. She has visited the Church of the Presentation in Philadelphia and is delighted to see what God is doing in our midst.*

God is doing as He promised, manifesting His glory throughout the Earth. Let us have high expectations as we enter more fully into the revival and as the revival unfolds.

Heavenly Father,

You have caused our expectation to be great concerning this coming revival. We expect Your arm to be made bare in the sight of all peoples and that Jesus shall be glorified.

In Your Name we pray,
Amen!

Responding
to
Revival Glory

Chapter 9

Staying in the Glory

And Moses said unto the LORD, See, thou sayest unto me, Bring up this people: and thou hast not let me know whom thou wilt send with me. Yet thou hast said, I know thee by name, and thou hast also found grace in my sight. Now therefore, I pray thee, if I have found grace in thy sight, show me now thy way, that I may know thee, that I may find grace in thy sight: and consider that this nation is thy people. And he said, My presence shall go with thee, and I will give thee rest. And he said unto him, If thy presence go not with me, carry us not up hence.

Exodus 33:12-15

If God is not with us, we don't want to be there. We might be in the finest gathering with the most exciting people. It might seem like the finest situation in the natural, but we simply don't want to be found anywhere without the presence of the Lord. Thank God that He is showing forth His presence in this day and hour.

God's presence is the glory. Farther down in the same chapter, Moses said:

> *I beseech thee, show me thy glory*   Verse 18

> *And the* LORD *said, Behold, there is a place by me, and thou shalt stand upon a rock: And it shall come to pass, while my glory passeth by, that I will put thee in a clift of the rock, and will cover thee with my hand while I pass by:*
>   Exodus 33:21-22

We're living in a different day. God is not just passing by. He's resting; He's abiding; He is causing us to live in His glory, His holy presence.

Jesus loved to go to Bethany. It was one of His favorite places. And the reason He liked to go there was that Mary, Martha and Lazarus loved to have Him in their home. There were, no doubt, other people in Bethany who wanted to be with Jesus because He was the Healer. There were those who wanted to be with Him because He was the Miracle Worker. He was the one that multiplied the loaves and the fishes, and some people loved Him for that. But Mary, Martha and Lazarus didn't require anything of the Master but His presence. "Please, just sit down," I hear one of them saying, "and allow us to prepare a meal for You. Sit here, and we will come and sit with You. We just want to visit with You. You don't need to give us any great teaching, just sit with us here in our house."

The Lord loves to be with those who reciprocate His love, those who love to be in His presence. This doesn't mean that God no longer delights to give miracles. He does. This doesn't mean that God no longer wants to heal. He does. But what we are beginning to learn is that there are miracles in His very presence. There is healing in His very presence. Without Him having to speak a word, a miracle can take place. His presence performs the miraculous. Without Him having to reach forth His hand and touch anyone, a miracle can take place. His presence produces miracles.

There is a glory in God's presence, and we are learning to appreciate that manifestation of His presence among us. I don't want to go to church where His presence is not manifested. The choir might be the finest; the sermon might be the greatest; but I would rather be in a place where the choir is not as musically gifted (as far as the world is concerned), but is made up of those who can sing in the glory and can bring the glory into my soul and into my spirit.

I love to be with those who gather to be with Him, for when it happens, suddenly His presence is felt tangibly among us. That's why I love to come to church. I never leave the House of the Lord without touching His glory because God has taught us how to get into that glory, how to experience it.

God said to Moses, *"There is a place by Me."* That's the place I want to be. That place is reserved for me, so that I can get near Him.

He says to us, *"Draw near."* It's like pulling up your chair and sitting next to your grandfather. It's like pulling up your chair and sitting next to your best friend. It's like pulling up your chair and sitting close to your closest brother. There is a drawing near unto the Lord that, in itself, is holy. There is a drawing near unto the Lord that, in itself, is righteous. Just getting near Him, you begin to feel His presence and the manifestation of His glory.

The glory affects you in tangible ways:

> *And it came to pass, when Moses came down from mount Sinai with the two tables of testimony in Moses' hand, when he came down from the mount, that Moses wist not that the skin of his face shone while he talked with him.*
>
> Exodus 34:29

The shine on the face of Moses was the evidence of the presence of God. You can't be in His presence without it becoming visible in your life. One night recently four Baptist people attended our service. They said the reason they came was that they saw such a dramatic change in their coworker, David Hunter, after he had attended our meetings.

The presence of the Lord changes us in every aspect of our being. It was seen as a shine on the face of Moses, and each of us must take on the glory look, a holy look, the look of one who has been gazing into the face of Jesus. You can often see it in people's eyes when they have been with God.

In a service in Caddo Mills, Texas, a mother and her son were among those who were slain in the Spirit. The young man laid there for an hour or more without moving, seemingly frozen in place. A night or two after I left, Sister Shelli Baker was still there ministering, and that particular night she laid hands on the young man and he, along with many others, fell out under the power of God. Several hours later, the pastor was getting ready to leave the church, and the young man was still lying there frozen in place in the Spirit.

Most of the lights in the auditorium had been dimmed, and suddenly the people who were still present noticed a light resting on the young man. But it was not just resting on him, it seemed to be radiating out from him, coming out of the very pores of his skin. I had always considered that the glory radiating from the face of Moses was a reflection, that because he had been standing face to face with the Lord, the light from the countenance of the Lord had shone onto Moses face, and that external experience had worked its way inward. After I heard about the experience of that young man in Texas, however, I'm not so sure. It seems to me now that it was an internal experience that worked its way out to the exterior.

Moses' face shone, and ours can too. How bright was it? It was not just a glow, not just a glimmer. It was brilliant. His face shone so brightly that the people were unable to look at him. That's what God wants to do for us in these days. We formerly thought that only Moses could have had such a great experience, but now we know that we are all destined to see the glory of God and to reflect it to the world.

Moses was in God's presence longer than most of us, but as we get into it more and more, spending time with Him, communing with Him, worshiping Him, we will find that the glorious light of the Gospel of Jesus Christ not only shines into our hearts, but shines forth from our lives as well.

I have a wonderful painting that is quite old, but has just recently been released. It is of the resurrected Lord in the garden on the morning of the resurrection. He is speaking with Mary. The artist has done a masterful job of capturing the moment, for there is such a glory on Mary's countenance, and something that I could only describe as the resurrection glory shining forth from the face of the Lord.

I know that there was a glory on Jesus throughout His earthly ministry. It was present at His birth. But on that resurrection morning, the glory that was upon Him was a greater glory than the glory manifested at the place of the nativity. There had been a glory upon

Him as He walked the Earth performing miracles, but this was an even greater glory. This was more like the glory that came upon Him on the Mount of Transfiguration, when God gave Him a foretaste of resurrection. The resurrected Christ is the One we serve and, as He went from glory to glory to glory, He is now taking us from one glory to a greater glory.

I was very blessed this year to have a wonderful vision of Jesus as the resurrected Lord. The thing that was so glorious about Him was that there was a life in the glory that surrounded Him as He came forth from the grave, a life in that glory beyond any glory I had witnessed before. For many days after that, every time I would even consider the resurrection and Jesus, the resurrected Lord, I would again see that wonderful life and that vibrant glory, a glory that was still alive. I was so blessed by it and, in fact, when I begin to talk about it now, I see again that resurrection glory.

Many of us are just now beginning to come into the experience that Moses had on the mount with God. It comes when we genuinely hunger for God's presence, when we cry out to Him, "Show me Your glory." Just as Jesus was changed before the eyes of the disciples, we are being changed by the manifestation of the glory of the Lord. He is changing us from glory to glory. These are revival days in which He is working those transforming graces into our lives, and He is doing it by the power of His Spirit.

I want to declare, as did Moses: if God's presence goes not with me, I just don't want to go. I don't want to go where He has not gone before me in the fullness of His glory, in that manifestation of His presence. He is causing the veil to be taken from our eyes, the blinders to fall away, the scales to drop. He is removing the hindrances and the limitations of our own minds and our own thinking, and is causing even the crust that has been upon our hearts through the cares of this life to be removed from us, that we might experience His glory in a new and greater way. He is revealing Himself unto us by the power of His Holy Spirit.

The day is upon us that when others look at us, they will see the visible glory of the Lord standing beside us. This is the glory that He desires to manifest in these days, so that some will say, "You didn't come alone." We may insist that we did indeed come alone, but they will insist with equal fervor that they have seen another.

If the people of Babylon could see the Fourth Man in the fiery furnace, God can cause the presence of a Second Person to be so real with us that others cannot deny His presence. He is with us in the midst of the circumstances of life, and we will sense His presence more and more in the days ahead.

There's nothing like the presence of the Lord. He is with us, not only by promise, but by experience. We can feel Him. The more we live in His presence the more determined we are, like Moses, that if His presence goes not with us, we ourselves will not go. We are determined to stay in the glory.

God is forcing us to have an upward look, sometimes through the situations of our lives. They are so difficult that we are forced to look up to God. Each of us must learn to look up into the glory, without having to be forced.

For twenty-five years we have lived in Jerusalem and, during that time, we have learned how to come into the presence of the Lord and be lifted up above current crises. That's the difference between the buzzard and the eagle. While the buzzard stays close to the earth, scanning the ground for dead flesh, the eagle rises above everything that is happening in this earthly realm and soars in high places. In the Spirit, God has given us that ability to soar.

In Jerusalem, over and over again, the news would be absolutely terrible. I have said many times that living with *"rumours of wars"* is worse than living with war, and I believe it.

War is not pleasant either. We lived through the Gulf War inside a sealed room. When we heard the sirens go off at two in the morning, we all jumped up quickly from our beds, rushed to the designated room, sealed the doors, put on our gas masks and sat down to see what would happen next. We were required to do all that in less than two minutes. However, this experience and all that went with it wasn't nearly as difficult as living with the constant rumors of war.

Nearly every day there was some rumor of impending disaster. "Before morning the Syrians will attack." "Before the week is out, we will have ... (this and that and the other)." At first, we found these rumors to be very disturbing. What if they were true? Certainly we wanted to be prepared. What should we do to prepare? How could we know exactly what would happen or how serious the crisis might prove to be?

We quickly learned that when we had heard such rumors, the best thing we could do was to get in the Spirit. It appears that sometimes the enemy doesn't realize that by sending so many troubles your way he is driving you into the arms of the Lord. If he is after you long enough, you will learn to get in the Spirit more quickly.

It's a lot like having an emergency drill. The first time you have the drill, it might take you fifteen minutes to accomplish it, but if you have it often enough, you will learn to cut that time considerably. We should be thankful for our problems that drive us to seek the Lord.

Every one of us must learn how to quickly come into the presence of the Lord and to roll all our heavy burdens off on Jesus. We must learn to look, not at the things which are temporal, but look up — at the things that are eternal.

God has given us an eternal hope. This is far greater

than the natural hope that is transient and passes with time. Because our hope is eternal, we must get caught up in the glory and see the eternal realms. We must allow God to lift us often into those realms by His Spirit.

When most people speak about the Lord being an All-Consuming Fire, they usually say it in reference to sins in their lives they are sure they need to repent of. While it's true that many of us have extra baggage we need to get rid of, those of us who are earnestly seeking God are living a sinless life. When we do make a mistake, the Holy Spirit is quick to convict us, and we quickly ask for forgiveness and go on. We're living sinless lives before God, but we do have weights that we're not willing to let go of until He consumes it by His fire. That's all He wants. He wants to have His fire burning in us until He becomes our every wish, our every thought, our every desire, our every plan, and our every purpose. He consumes us and permeates our very being, until the vision of the Lord is totally with us, totally upon us.

You might say, "But, Sister Ruth, we live in a natural world." Yes, we do, but we don't have to be touched by it. Our feet can be touching this natural world, or our hands can be touching natural situations, while, at the same time, we can be soaring in the heavenlies.

It's not your paper work or your job that is pulling you down. It is the limitation of your thought life.

God's fire can so consume you that you can fulfill all your earthly obligations and not be held captive by any of them. Get in the glory and stay in the glory, and the earthly things will take care of themselves.

Heavenly Father,

How wonderful is Your presence! How delighted we are to live in Your presence! How thankful we are that You go with us, even to the end of the age.

Amen!

Chapter 10

Moving in the Glory

And when the cloud was taken up from over the tabernacle, the children of Israel went onward in all their journeys: But if the cloud were not taken up, then they journeyed not till the day that it was taken up. Exodus 40:36-37

And when the cloud was taken up from the tabernacle, then after that the children of Israel journeyed: and in the place where the cloud abode, there the children of Israel pitched their tents. At the commandment of the LORD the children of Israel journeyed, and at the commandment of the LORD they pitched: as long as the cloud abode upon the tabernacle they rested in their tents.
And when the cloud tarried long upon the tabernacle many days, then the children of Israel kept the charge of the LORD, and journeyed not. And so it was, when the cloud was a few days upon the tabernacle; according to the commandment of the LORD they abode in their tents, and according to the commandment of the LORD they journeyed.

*And so it was, when the cloud abode from even
unto the morning, and that the cloud was taken
up in the morning, then they journeyed: whether
it was by day or by night that the cloud was taken
up, they journeyed. Or whether it were two days,
or a month, or a year, that the cloud tarried upon
the tabernacle, remaining thereon, the children
of Israel abode in their tents, and journeyed not:
but when it was taken up, they journeyed. At the
commandment of the LORD they rested in the
tents, and at the commandment of the LORD they
journeyed: they kept the charge of the LORD, at
the commandment of the LORD by the hand of
Moses.*   Numbers 9:17-23

The moving cloud was a very strange phenomenon
which the children of Israel experienced on their way
to the promised land. When they settled in one place,
it was because the glory was there. In that place, they
were blessed — because of the glory; in that place,
things went well — because of the glory. When the
cloud lifted, it would not have been unusual for them
to want to stay in that place of blessing. But the blessing is not in a place; it's in the cloud; it's in God's
presence.

The cloud was the visible sign of God's presence,
just as glory is the manifested presence of God with
us today. Sometimes they saw the cloud and sometimes they didn't, and glory can be visible or invisible.

It comes by revelation. The cloud was a tangible sign of change, just as the glory cloud is for us. The cloud was equivalent to the spoken commandment of the Lord, a visible sign of the spoken Word of God.

The people, I'm sure, often could not understand just why they should move on. They were so obviously in the will of God — at the right place, at the right time, and in the right circumstances. Why were they now being left without a cloud? And there are people all over America and around the world today who are sitting where they have been sitting for many years. They believe they are sitting under the cloud and don't even realize that the cloud has moved on. They got absorbed in the place where the cloud dwelt in former times and didn't see it lifting and moving on.

Many lovely Christians find themselves sitting in a beautiful tabernacle that once knew the glory, once knew the presence of God and once knew His revelation. They are now in consternation, wondering why they are not feeling the glory as before. If they had only been looking up, they might have seen the glory moving on. But they were too wrapped up in their surroundings to discern that God was doing a new thing.

Some people may stay where they are now for a very long time, for they have enough material to sustain them as they were. They can continue, as if the cloud were present, but they are only deceiving themselves. The cloud has moved on.

Trying to do anything without God's presence is what Paul meant when he wrote to the Corinthians:

> *I am become as sounding brass, or a tinkling cymbal.* 1 Corinthians 13:1

None of us enjoys being in a service where people are speaking the same truths they have spoken for many years, yet we cannot feel the glory of God in what they are saying.

At the beginning of the Toronto blessing, people traveled to that city from many parts of the world to be blessed. Friends of mine were attending a church in Australia where some of the leaders of the church had been to Toronto and had begun saturation services when they got back home. When I asked my friends what they thought of it, the husband replied first, "Well, some good things are happening. God is honoring the prayers of the leaders, and people are falling under the power of the Spirit."

"But, Ruth," the wife added, "Somehow the whole thing lacks that gorgeous feeling." In that one statement, she was letting us know that a certain form of revival had come to the church, but the glory was still somehow not present. She knew it by the lack of "that gorgeous feeling." In the glory there is a wonderful sense of the presence of God.

Sometimes, when we plan a great convention, it is difficult to know who to invite for speakers. Some of those we have known and enjoyed in days gone by are still speaking in the same old way, but their words now have a ring of insincerity to them. Known names are not always those who are flowing in the revelation of the hour. It is sometimes better to use new and inexperienced people who realize they know nothing and seek God with all their hearts for a fresh revelation than to use the old crowd-drawing people who have not kept up with the move of the glory cloud. The ability to draw a crowd is not an indication that someone is living under the cloud of God's glory.

We must learn to sense the moving of the cloud and learn to sense the glory upon a person. We cannot afford to stick with someone just because of a former greatness. It is time to move on. Move with the cloud.

Old revelation does not inspire the soul to greatness. Old revelation does not move us to excellence. Old revelation has the effect of putting us to sleep. We don't want to live any longer in old revelation. Move on if you want to live under the cloud, for it is moving.

We all repeat wonderful old stories. We all tell things that God did for us in the past. That's okay, but if, in the midst of the telling, God doesn't speak something new into our spirits for that particular day and that particular service, we are missing out on what He is doing in this day.

I, for one, am not satisfied to know that I have developed a lovely camp site. I am not satisfied with
the strength of the stakes I have driven into the surrounding soil. I am satisfied only with the glory, and
if the glory moves on, I must move with it, or my soul
will not be satisfied and at peace.

If we need to pull up stakes in order to keep up
with the glory cloud, then so be it. Get yourself a better stake puller so you can do it more quickly.

Yes, I believe your stakes need to be driven well
and that your tent needs to be secure. Yes, I believe in
permanence, and I want you to stay where you are
just as long as God wants you there. But be careful.
Don't let the glory cloud move on without you.

Moving is not always easy. It involves pulling up
stakes, packing things up and lightening the load. But
whatever you must do to rise up and follow the cloud
of glory that is moving on, do it. The wheel within
the wheel is turning. Don't miss what God is doing
because of something upon which you have set your
affections. Hold lightly the things of this world, and
be ready to move on with the cloud at a moment's
notice.

If you feel the fire within the fire burning, don't
hesitate. Don't turn aside for anything of this world.
Move on. If you sense the glory rising, you must rise
with it. If you sense the cloud moving on, you must
move on with it.

It doesn't matter if you just got your stakes down

like you wanted them. The move of God doesn't happen according to your timing. God cannot always accommodate your schedule. He moves sovereignly, as He wills, and if you don't move with Him, you will be left behind.

Learn to live under the cloud and not let anything cause you to come out from under it. Let it be under you and over you, so that you are encased in it, enveloped by it, and consumed by it. Be clothed with the glory cloud of God's Spirit.

The cloud is so all-consuming that in the days ahead we will see ministries that have resisted certain aspects of the move of God's Spirit in the past now being baptized in the cloud and doing things they never imagined themselves doing. Lord, hasten the day. Oh, move with the cloud.

It may seem to some like a hard statement to say that some churches don't know that the glory cloud is no longer with them. We must remember, however, that Mary and Joseph, such sincere, holy people that they were chosen by God to protect the Lord Jesus while He was in this world, had been traveling for some time without realizing that He was no longer with their company. He wasn't there, and they didn't even know it. When they realized it, only after several days, they turned back to Jerusalem to find Him. They had journeyed on with confidence, but His presence was not with them. He had stayed, while they had left.

Whether He moves on and we stay put, or we move on and He stays put, either way we're in trouble. We can't live without Him. May God make us to realize when it happens so that we can turn back to find Him.

Some people are never available when God wants to move on. If they don't have something "really important" to do first, they will think of something "really important" to do. So they miss God's best for their lives — every time.

God is tired of waiting on some people. If you have that spirit of always wanting things to happen in your time, you need to shake yourself and get up and run after God's glory. There is too much to lose. Get over your willfulness. It's not going to happen in your way and in your time. God is God, and when His chariot is moving on, you must move with it.

You may feel like you just got things ordered as you wanted them, that you were finally able to put some finishing touches on your dwelling place and to decorate it as you have wanted to for so long, only to see the cloud lifting and beginning to move away. This is a painful experience for many. Just when they think they have gotten their life under control, God is moving again, and things are changing.

If you are one of those people, what can you do? You have no alternative. You must follow the cloud. Give up what you have to give up; give away what you have to give away; sell what you have to sell; but move on with the glory cloud. Don't let anything or anybody hold you back. There is no other alternative.

If the presence of God is not with you in what you are doing, turn back to find Him. If His presence has gone on ahead, and you have not realized it, rise up and go quickly after Him. Don't delay.

If you have been sidetracked by trying a particular method that has borne fruit for someone else, turn back to find the Lord's presence. He is more important than a method, a system, or a program. Come back to the simplicity of His presence.

Under the cloud is the only place of safety. It is the only place of divine health. It is the only place of guaranteed provision. It is the only place of sure revelation. It is the only place which guarantees us salvation for our households and for our nation.

When the glory cloud began to move, the people of Israel had to quickly pack up their belongings, often, no doubt, having to lighten the load, so that they could move on. Whatever it takes, that's what we want to do.

When God poured His Spirit upon the disciples in the Upper Room, in just a few days time the structure of the spiritual movement was totally changed and God had raised up an entirely new group of leaders, those who trusted the Spirit of God. If people have become static, if they are exactly where they have been for some time, if they haven't changed in twenty years, I would consider them in danger of being passed over.

God is moving on. He tells me frequently, "Ruth, when I get finished with you, you won't recognize yourself." And I believe it. He has changed me again and again. And He is changing me more every day.

Revival is spontaneous, and we must learn to be spontaneous. For many years I took my concordance with me to the platform because, as I waited in the presence of God in my seat, He would drop a word into my heart. Then I would look up that scripture and know His message for the hour. Now, however, God sometimes waits to give me my sermon until I'm already standing in the pulpit, so I usually take my concordance with me to the podium. This is a new day.

Sometimes I start prophesying, and while I am prophesying, the direction of the sermon comes to me. I love spontaneity and God does too.

That doesn't mean that God can't speak to us before the time to preach. He can. But I know that He is looking for people who will let Him flow by His Spirit.

Sometimes we need to stop every other activity and listen carefully to what the Spirit is saying. We can get so busy that we don't even notice that we are being left behind. Stop every other activity and become sensitive to the glory cloud. Then, when it starts to move, rise up and go quickly after it.

Some people are distressed about any kind of change, but that's foolish. God has given us His Word, and we know the intents of His heart. He has but one desire for us, and that one desire is that we be changed from glory to glory. He has never moved a person to a lesser glory than they've already experienced. Change, therefore, is our friend. The changes God is sending into our lives are intended to work in us *"a far more exceeding and eternal weight of glory."* In fact, change becomes the measure of the glory.

It doesn't take long to get ready once one is convinced that moving is the right thing to do. It's the decisions that take a long time. The moving itself doesn't take very long. Getting in the frame of mind necessary for moving is much more difficult than the moving process itself. Put aside every excuse and begin to move with the cloud of God's glory.

After my brother died, I decided to move into his house since it was given to both of us many years ago. I was in no hurry. There were some changes to be made to it, and I was comfortable right where I was.

One morning I wanted to make a telephone call from my room, but when I picked up the receiver, I discovered that the line was dead. There had been a miscommunication with the phone company and my line had been prematurely disconnected so that it could be changed to the house. I jiggled the phone and checked the connection, at the phone and at the wall outlet, but it was truly dead.

When I sent someone to the camp office to call the phone company, they understood that the house connection would be made immediately, so I suddenly decided that it was moving day. I had been putting off that decision for a long time, but it was suddenly made for me.

We like to make our own decisions, but it is easier and safer for us to let God make them. Moving was easy for me, because I developed the habit, through many years of traveling for the Lord, of keeping a small suitcase packed and waiting by the door. When I get back home from one trip, I take out the dirty clothes and put in some clean ones and keep that suitcase ready for the next time. All I have to do is pick up a couple of toiletry items from the dresser, grab some clothes on hangers from the closet, and I'm ready to go out the door. It took me about ten minutes to move. There were still some things that I would have to sort through at a future time, but I was moved.

When I got over to the house I discovered that there was no coffee and no coffee maker and nothing else to drink. I would have preferred to do it the opposite way, to get ready first and then move, but God didn't let me do it that way. God wants us to start moving, and He will put things in order as we do. When we get in order, then the things around us will get in order.

When God shows you that it is moving time, it may not seem like a convenient day or a convenient time. God is nudging us to get into the fullness of the flow of the river of God.

The more you touch the heavenly, the more you

know the glory realm, the more you want to know it, reaching in beyond anything that we have known or experienced. If we are willing, God will help us make a quicker shift from the old to the new.

There is a transition period in which we have a mixture of old and new. Sometimes we have more of the old than the new, and other times more of the new than the old. But God is helping us to flow into those greater realms of His glory, not just having spurts of it, touches of it, and glimpses of it, but rivers of it.

Let us be lifted up into realms of glory that we have never before experienced. I will not be satisfied with anything less, and I know you won't either.

There is a rhythm to the glory, and when we speak of the glory cloud we speak of moving. Even when the glory cloud remained still, those who were under it were moving. They were moving from one realm to another realm, from one dimension to another dimension, from one authority to another authority, and from one glory to another glory. We must learn to sit under the glory cloud, and when that glory cloud begins to move, we must rise up and move on with it.

All of those who are sensing the cloud of glory in their lives are also experiencing a sense of acceleration in the movement of events around them. Historically, the cloud moved only every few decades or every few years, and the people of God sensed a change in what He was doing. Today, however, we are experiencing many sudden and unexpected changes. Sometimes we camp one night thinking that we have settled down for a while. But no sooner have we settled in than the cloud lifts and begins to move on. If we are not to be left behind, we must quickly strike our tents and rush to keep up with the moving cloud.

The cloud never goes backward. When God lifts us into a new realm of glory, He has shown us that it is important never to go back to the former realm. Move in the cloud and move with the cloud. Get to know the movings of the Spirit, with the cloud over you, with the cloud under you, with the cloud surrounding you. When you are moving with the cloud, you have nothing to worry about.

Father,

Let us be lifted up into realms we have never known before. Let us be taught of the Spirit. Let the Heavens be opened unto us. Let Your glory be with us, and let us understand Your glory cloud and how to live under it continually. Take from us all fear of moving on, for we know that the place into which You lead us is the place of blessing. We, therefore, are determined to move on with You into the new.

In Jesus' name,
Amen!

Chapter 11

Being Carried Away in the Glory

After this I looked, and, behold, a door was opened in heaven: and the first voice which I heard was as it were of a trumpet talking with me; which said, Come up hither, and I will show thee things which must be hereafter. And immediately I was in the spirit; and, behold, a throne was set in heaven, and one sat on the throne.

Revelation 4:1-2

When John heard the Lord calling him to come up higher, he was *"immediately ... in the Spirit."* John was carried away in the Spirit, an experience that we are having more and more these days. One minute John was on the Isle of Patmos, looking at his earthly surroundings, and the next minute he was *"in Heaven"* looking at *"the throne."*

John didn't have to take himself anywhere. He just had to yield to the Spirit and the Spirit carried him away. The place commonly identified as John's shelter while on the Isle of Patmos was not very elaborate. It was a simple cave. But when John was carried away, and he opened his eyes, he was no longer in a cave. He was in the presence of God.

Ezekiel had a similar experience. He said:

> *The hand of the LORD was upon me, and carried me out in the spirit of the LORD, and set me down in the midst of the valley.*   Ezekiel 37:1

The *"hand of the Lord"* is able to come upon us in these days and *"carry [us] away"* as well. This carrying away is wonderful because God Himself chooses the itinerary. When we choose, we can sometimes be disappointed, but when God chooses, we are never disappointed. He is sovereign God, and when He carries us away, we're not sure where we are going.

John was taken directly to the throne and began to see it in all its glory. He saw what was in front of it, what was behind it, and what was around it. God may carry you to some other place and there show you His purposes to drop faith into your heart to believe for the greater thing, to teach you in realms that you have never known. God does not want us to be earthbound. We were not designed for this world, and when we are caught up in the Spirit, He lets us know, in a way that we could not know otherwise, that we are only pilgrims here on this Earth, that we are not natural, but spiritual.

In the moments when the glory is manifested, ordinary people like you and I are suddenly carried away and permitted to see things that are not visible to the physical eye. Just as there is natural seeing, there is spiritual seeing. Some people are teaching us that we should picture what we want God to do and believe Him for it, but I prefer to let God choose for me. I let Him give me the vision, rather than me trying to give Him the vision. I could never imagine things as glorious as He shows me. I could never even begin to dream of all that is in the heart of God for me. My own expectations are so small in comparison to His expectations for me.

Get your head into the river. Let the river touch your hearing; let it touch your seeing; let it touch your reasoning faculties; let it touch every part of your life. There has never been a day of revelation like this day. *Ordinary people are seeing things that only great people knew of in days gone by:*

> *For verily I say unto you, That many prophets and righteous men have desired to see those things which ye see, and have not seen them; and to hear those things which ye hear, and have not heard them.* Matthew 13:17

> *Out of the mouth of babes and sucklings hast thou ordained strength because of thine enemies, that thou mightest still the enemy and the avenger.* Psalm 8:2

In order to be carried away in the glory, you must first learn to yield yourself to the Spirit. The Apostle Paul wrote:

> *Neither yield ye your members as instruments*
> *of unrighteousness unto sin: but yield yourselves*
> *unto God, as those that are alive from the dead,*
> *and your members as instruments of righteous-*
> *ness unto God.* Romans 6:13

It's all in the yielding. You can get into the river just as quickly as you want to. You can get into the glory just as quickly as you want to. If you are hungry enough, you'll yield. You don't need five more evangelists to come by and lead you out gently. Just get in. Let the river carry you out.

Paul continued:

> *I speak after the manner of men because of the*
> *infirmity of your flesh: for as ye have yielded your*
> *members servants to uncleanness and to iniquity*
> *unto iniquity; even so now yield your members*
> *servants to righteousness unto holiness.*
> Romans 6:19

We know more about yielding than we care to let on. All of our lives we have yielded ourselves as instruments of sin. All of our lives we have yielded ourselves as instruments of iniquity. The yielding is the same; it's just the purpose that has changed now. Some people have danced in the world, but they are hesitant to dance in the Spirit for fear that they will be "in the flesh." If you could yield yourself in that sinful world, you can yield yourself in the holy world, too.

Drawing near to God is a holy act, and if you are drawing nigh to Him through dancing, or if you are drawing nigh to Him by the uplifted hand, no matter how you are drawing nigh unto God, that very yielding unto Him is holy. Yield yourself to Him and let Him carry you to places you could only dream of otherwise.

We are all learning to yield our members unto the Lord. Usually it doesn't matter to me if people fall out or not, but occasionally there is somebody that I put my hand on, and I sense that they are resisting the flow of God. Most of the time I just pray twice and move on to others, but sometimes I feel constrained by the Holy Spirit to help them.

Some people start walking backward, trying not to fall. I say to them, "Stand still and yield to the Holy Ghost." When they stand still, they go down. At other times, when I see someone standing there, waiting for the Spirit to knock them down, I say to them, "Just yield to the Spirit like you would yield yourself to your father's arms." Or, sometimes I might say, "Let the river carry you. Just float on the river." When they do, they are suddenly carried away on the river.

Knowing how to yield our members to God is not always automatic. We have to learn it. God can operate on us as a surgeon would operate while we are sitting or while we are standing, but He often lays us down so that He can teach us the new. To learn the new we must relax in God's river and float in the glory. Relax your members and yield them to God. You may not know what He will do through you in the future, but trust Him, and don't be afraid.

If you are the type who has to have everything proven to you over and over again before you will try it yourself, you may find yourself on the sidelines watching others move ahead. If others just swim on out, without having to wait until everything is proven to them, they will quickly pass you by. If they are willing to yield themselves to God and let Him do what He wants, while you sit around and argue about it, you will quickly get behind in the flow of the revival.

Once you have spoken in tongues the first time, it is much easier after that. You know how to yield to it. Once you have laughed in the Spirit the first time, it is much easier after that. You know how to yield to it and you can do it over and over again. Yield your members to God.

Sometimes it's your hands that God wants you to yield, sometimes it's your feet and sometimes it's your lips.

If you don't think it is important to swim, you will never try it. If you think you are doing just fine without it, you will never put forth the effort necessary to learn. Beholding the river is wonderful, but the river is for swimming, not just for beholding. Describing the river is wonderful, but this river is not just for describing, it is for swimming. Don't just talk about it. Get out into its waters and start swimming. Many people who are preaching lovely sermons on the river haven't taken time to learn to swim in it yet. What are you waiting for?

God is saying, "Get out there and swim. These are *'waters to swim in.'* " I don't know about you, but I'm ready to swim. Not only am I ready to swim, but I am also ready to learn some new strokes.

Joy will give us the strength that we need for the swimming. Long-distance swimmers train and train some more to be able to endure the most grueling races, but we can swim across channels because of the joy of the Lord that is birthed in us. God gives us strength for the long term, for all that we will face in this last day and hour.

God, our Coach, does not stand on the bank shouting instruction to us, but He is with us in the depths of the river, beckoning unto us, encouraging us, strengthening us. We hear His voice constantly urging us, "Come out farther. Come on out. Launch out into the deep." He goes before us and is our Instructor and Helper in all our ways. Multitudes are getting into these waters. Don't be left behind. Move on out.

Be bold! Be daring! Swim on out. Don't worry what will happen to you in the deep water. Trust God. Swim on out. Jump out into the middle of this stream.

Last summer Ruthie Kendrick did a black and white

photo study of our campmeeting and the glory of the Lord we experienced. She had decided that instead of traveling in Europe or some other place, she would spend her summer photographing revival. At first she considered going to Pensacola and photographing what God was doing there. Later, she thought of several other places. In the end, she decided to stay right here in the Richmond area and to document what God was doing in her own hometown.

When the new library at Saint Catherine's School in Richmond was dedicated, with an illustrious guest list, Ruthie's Glory exhibition was on display, photos of God pouring out His power on humble people under the Tabernacle in Ashland, Virginia. When I had seen the lovely photos, I called my good friend Carolyn Duncan and asked if she would publish them in a book. She agreed to do it so that the world could be blessed by them, too. What a nice thing to have, a photographic album of God's people being carried away in the glory.

Lord,

I want to be carried away, again and again, into heavenly realms, again and again. I want to be carried away with You.

In Jesus' name,
Amen! Amen!

Chapter 12

Trusting the Glory for Provision

But my God shall supply all your need according to his riches in glory by Christ Jesus.

Philippians 4:19

When we become a praising people, a people of the glory cloud, we will find our needs automatically supplied. I don't want to know the throne of God only as a place of petition. I no longer enjoy services that are predominantly need-oriented. They are too focused on people and not on God. I know that God's people have needs, but I don't want to spend my time concentrating on lacks and needs, and I don't want to preach and minister in such a way as to keep people focused in this way either. We can become totally consumed with problems, sickness, financial want, emotional problems, etc., and miss the great things God wants to do for us. Our God is great, and we must not spend all our time concerned for physical, material needs.

There is provision in the cloud of God's glory just as the natural cloud gives provision for the earth:

For as the rain cometh down, and the snow from heaven, and returneth not thither, but watereth the earth, and maketh it bring forth and bud, that it may give seed to the sower, and bread to the eater: Isaiah 55:10

Stop looking at the things that are seen. Stop going over and over your budget, trying to figure out how it's all going to be possible. That's an act of unbelief. There are some things that you don't want to examine too closely. Just get the overall picture. You don't need to be frightened by the details. Keep your eyes on the heavenlies. See the eternal, the invisible, things of God.

Some fail to move with the glory cloud because they think that a cloud has no substance and that there is nothing practical in it. How foolish! We don't need anything more substantial than the cloud of God's glory. That's as substantial as you can get. If you have nothing else, you can leave home based on the moving of the cloud. In recent years I have stayed in some of the most beautiful homes in the world. I would have to call them mansions. God does it just like He promised:

And every one that hath forsaken houses, or brethren, or sisters, or father, or mother, or wife, or children, or lands, for my name's sake, shall re-

*ceive an hundredfold, and shall inherit everlast-
ing life.* Matthew 19:29

You have nothing to fear when you are following
the cloud of God's glory. That cloud is so substantial
that it can cause you to leave every other security behind, and you will know that it is enough. As long as
you are conscious that the cloud is over your head,
and as long as you are willing to rise up when it begins to move and to hold still when it stops, you have
nothing to worry about financially. God will do for
you the things He has appointed.

You don't need to have resources in order for God
to use you these days. Just get under His cloud, and
He will take care of the rest. You don't need to be famous in order to be used by God. You just need to
get under His glory cloud. He can put you at the forefront of situations, just as easily as He can put another
person there, and He can provide for your needs just
as easily as He can provide for another.

What God is doing for His people in this last day
and hour is astounding. He spoke to us one day and
said, "One moment it won't be, and the next moment
it will be," and it's happening. One moment there is
nothing, and the next moment there is much. One
moment there is no opportunity, and the next moment
there is great opportunity. One moment nothing
seems to be happening, and the next moment so much
is happening that we can't seem to keep up with it.
Oh, get under the cloud, for it's beginning to move.

If God has opened a door for you in the Spirit, you don't need any other open door. His glory is sufficient. If you insist on having something "more substantial," you will miss the will of God for your life. Stop asking God for something "more substantial" and start asking Him to make you sensitive to the cloud of His glory. Ask Him to let you see it and feel it and move with it. Ask Him to teach you when the glory is present and when it is not. Ask Him to make you more alert to the changes of the moment. Ask Him to help you to know how to rise up when the cloud rises. Ask Him to teach you how to bring the cloud into the midst of the congregation. If you will be faithful to do that, you have nothing to worry about with respect to finances.

An Indian couple came to visit our camp one summer. They had planned to travel, raising money for their work in India, but the Lord spoke to them to stay at camp, to stay in the glory and to receive more and more of Him. While they were in the campmeeting, they gave the last four hundred dollars they had in the offerings. When their time was up and they returned to their country, they were not laden down with material blessings, as they had anticipated when they planned their trip to America, but they were laden down with spiritual blessings.

They hadn't been home very long before a letter came from someone they had never met and didn't know, and it contained a check for twenty-four thousand dollars. The couple was rather shocked, to say the least, and decided to call the party who sent the check, to thank them and to know what had motivated them to send such a large amount of money. Where had their benefactors gotten their name and address? And how did they know there was a need in their particular ministry?

When they were able to speak with the people who sent the check, they were told that the Lord had given them the name and address through prayer and told them to send this exact amount of money. You never lose financially by moving with the cloud and resting under it.

A lovely pastor came and sat beside me in a meeting in Caddo Mills, Texas. I was refreshed by his excitement. He said, "I had a visitation from an angel, a messenger from the Lord. I was told that God had chosen my church to be one of those that would experience revival. I was sure this couldn't happen, for several important reasons, and I told the angel as much."

"First, I told the angel, this couldn't happen because my church building was much too small. We only had pews for about a hundred people, a hundred and fifty at the most.

"The angel said, 'We can take care of that.' " The Father wants all churches, both big and small, to experience revival.

" 'Well, okay,' I answered, 'but the revival can't happen in my church because I don't have anybody to help me.' The angel reminded me that four new people had just come into the church. 'Each of those,' he showed me, 'is able to help you with revival.' "

" 'Okay,' I accepted that, but I was still sure that this couldn't happen to my church because we had no money."

" 'We can take care of that,' the angel assured me again."

"Then I was sure that revival couldn't come to our church because our parking facility was so limited, but that didn't seem to be a problem for the angel. He told me to go to the church every day and pray for an hour and a half, in addition to what I was already doing, to invite my staff to come and pray with me, but not to insist if they seemed reluctant to do it.

"I began to go to the church and pray an hour and a half each day, and, one by one, my staff members began to join me. And, very soon revival began to break out in our services."

Before long, a church that was closing its doors called this pastor to say that they had some money they wanted to give him, and they gave him thirty thousand dollars, which enabled him to pave some parking space around the church. Then they called him to say they had eight musical instruments they wanted to give him.

He was able to raise money to buy two hundred and fifty folding chairs. The pews the church had used had limited their seating capacity. Chairs would take up less space, so he could get more people in by using them. In this way, his capacity was nearly doubled.

All this had taken place in only a few weeks, and now the brother said to me, "Sister Ruth, I have a serious problem. I feel like I have taken my people as far as I know how to take them. What do I do now?"

I said, "Brother, anyone who has had a visitation from an angel doesn't need me to tell him how to do it." I did become carnal and suggested that he buy my *Glory* book, telling him that it would help his people come into greater realms of glory.

I was so thrilled to hear this simple story of God's provision that I have repeated the story a number of times in my preaching. This is typical of what God is doing all over the world. We have absolutely nothing to fear in the realm of provision when we get into the cloud of God's glory.

God's pattern of provision for my own life and ministry was established when I was still very young. I had promised God when I was fifteen years old that if He would provide for me, I would never take a secular job or receive a salary. I was living in Hong Kong and receiving only about fifty dollars a month for my support, when a door opened for me to minister in India. Many of the Indian leaders invited American evangelists to come and preach but expected them, before coming, to raise thousands of dollars in America to pay for the expenses of the crusades. Some friends of mine had spent months raising funds for a single crusade, and I didn't want to do that.

I was sure there must be people in ministry in India who were praying for preachers and ministers for some upcoming conference or large meeting. I prayed that I would be the answer to their prayers and that God would put me in contact with them supernaturally, and that's exactly what He did.

God led me to Pastor P.M. Phillip in Kottayam, Kerala, one of India's greatest evangelists, and a man who was regularly invited to speak at the largest conventions in India. I was taken to his annual convention at the Town Hall in Kottayam. After testifying, he invited me to stay on and be the evening speaker at the conference. I was about twenty-one at the time. I was then privileged to share the platform with him during six months of the year for four consecutive years, preaching with him and on my own at the major conventions to many thousands of people. Among the conventions where I preached was the famous All-India Pentecostal Convention.

All this ministry in India never cost me a cent. I did share with the Indian brethren whatever finances God gave me, but I didn't have the great burden of raising large sums of money for specific meetings. It was God's provision for me at the time and a pattern for things to come. Throughout my life I have watched as God has repeated this miracle for me over and over again.

I have learned to trust Him daily for provision all these years. Whether it has been a small thing that I needed or a large financial miracle, I have known the miraculous provision of the Lord day by day and have been just as grateful for the dollar as for the hundred dollars. It is all God's faithfulness and the faithfulness of God's people.

Two weeks before my brother went to Heaven Sister Ruth Carneal and I were ministering at the church that Renee Smith attends in Lincolnton, Georgia. Ruth was speaking words of knowledge over the congregation when she suddenly turned to me and said, "I just saw you in vision holding two very deep offering bags. God is going to increase you in freewill offerings.

I had lived all my life and ministry by offerings and didn't realize until after my brother's death the reason for that message. God had been so faithful in letting me know that the offering bags would be deeper and fuller to take care of the new challenges I would be facing.

Get in the Spirit, and God will provide for you, too. *He* is all you need.

Lord,

You are all we need for body, soul and spirit. In You is the fullness of provision. Cause us to live in the reality of the riches of Your glory.

In Jesus' name,
Amen!

Chapter 13

Resting in the Glory

Thus were the journeyings of the children of Is-rael according to their armies, when they set forward. And Moses said ... We are journeying unto the place of which the LORD said, I will give it you: come thou with us, and we will do thee good: for the LORD hath spoken good concerning Israel.
Numbers 10:28-29

And they departed from the mount of the LORD three days' journey: and the ark of the covenant of the LORD went before them in the three days' journey, to search out a resting place for them. And the cloud of the LORD was upon them by day, when they went out of the camp. And it came to pass, when the ark set forward, that Moses said, Rise up, LORD, and let thine enemies be scattered; and let them that hate thee flee before thee. And when it rested, he said, Return, O LORD, unto the many thousands of Israel.
Numbers 10:33-36

I am convinced that God wants to bring us into a realm of glory where we know His rest. He wants all the struggle and striving within us to fall away. He has a place of rest for us, a place of confidence, and it is to be found in His glory.

We could never find this resting place on our own, but God goes before us and searches out this place of rest. Then we can sit beside His river and rest, knowing that He will supply our every need.

We may come into the sanctuary with the distresses of life upon us, but within a few moments spent in God's glory, we are rested. We feel as if we have had a month's vacation, and we suddenly understand *"the peace of God which passeth all understanding."* We don't need the psychiatrist's couch. We don't even need the hours of counseling sessions with church leaders. In the glory realm, we find the Lord going before us and searching out a resting place for us, leading us into that realm where we may find rest for our souls.

Not only does the Lord go before us and find a resting place in the spiritual realm, but if we enter into that Spirit realm, we will find that He is searching out every area of our lives. We don't have to plan every moment of our ministries. God is doing it for us — by His Spirit. Just move into the place of revelation, and He will speak, and you will know that what He is saying is the answer for you.

One of my concerns about coming back to minister in America was that I didn't want to lose the touch we had gained by traveling the nations for many years by revelation. Many Americans are much too organized and programmed well into the future, and I just want to be led step by step by the Spirit.

In April, just prior to speaking at the Pastor's Conference in Brownsville, Brother Batchelor called me and said, "I told my congregation that I was going to take you home with me from the Pastor's Conference."

"Where do you live?" I asked.

And he replied, "I live in Alabama, about two hours away from Pensacola."

I asked him, "What do you have in mind?" and when he told me, I decided to go with him. We had a Friday night service with his people and then a lunch with some of the local pastors on Saturday and services on Saturday night and Sunday. On our way to the lunch on Saturday, I remembered that I hadn't called home to let our staff know where I was, so I quickly called the camp office and left the number of the motel where I was staying.

When I got back from the lunch, there was a message waiting for me. When I returned the call, a gentleman answered: "Sister Ruth," he said, "I'm Jerry Stuart. I'm a pastor, and I read your book a few weeks ago. I was so challenged that I started having meetings every night with my people, and we've been going on now every night for the last two weeks. I would really appreciate it if you could find time to come and minister to us."

I asked, "Where are you?"

He told me that he was in Stockbridge, south of Atlanta, and I found that very interesting because I was planning to be in the Benny Hinn crusade in Atlanta beginning that next Thursday. I had planned to fly to Dallas at the beginning of the week to visit friends while I was so near, but I hadn't had time to let them know I was coming and hadn't made an airline reservation yet. "If you are willing," I told him, "I could be there for Monday, Tuesday and Wednesday nights."

"That's what God told me you would say," he replied.

I don't know if he was happier because I was coming or if I was happier because God was leading my steps, but we were both thrilled with the arrangement. The Lord had done it with such ease. I had a wonderful time with Pastor Jerry Stuart, his wife and congregation at their church. Then, we attended the Benny Hinn crusade together.

About noon on Thursday, a pastor from Macon, Georgia, called me at the motel. Two ladies from his church had attended the meetings in Stockbridge. He was inviting me to Macon to minister. In the course of the conversation I asked him if he was coming up to Atlanta for the Benny Hinn crusade beginning that night. He had not planned to come; however, I told him how important it is to be in the collective anointing of twenty thousand people praising and worshiping together. Healings and miracles happen so easily in a corporate anointing. I personally love the excitement for Jesus that is generated in such a gathering. The atmosphere becomes charged by the presence of God.

Within a few minutes I had talked him into joining me for the evening service. He was at the church. He called his wife to prepare his clothing and the intercessors in the church began to pray as he began the five-hour drive to Atlanta. Those next three services were life-changing for him.

In the fall of 1996, I was invited to speak at the Ladies Convention for the Assembly of God Church in Fargo, North Dakota. The morning of the final day of meetings, as I was leaving my seat and walking to the pulpit, the Lord spoke to me and said that He was *"sit[ting] upon the flood."* I did not fully perceive what this meant.

My associate, Sister Ruth Carneal, had been addressing the assembly before me and told how the old song "Red River Valley" kept coming to her mind. When she mentioned it to the convention organizer, she was told that we were actually in the Red River Valley. We hadn't known that fact.

I sensed such an awe in what God was saying to me, that He was *"sit[ting] upon the flood,"* that I immediately began to cry. I quickly located the verse where that phrase is used and read it:

*The LORD sitteth upon the flood; yea, the LORD
sitteth King for ever.*   Psalms 29:10

The following April we were scheduled to speak at
a Praise, Worship and Glory Conference at the same
church in Fargo. It was the day before the terrible flood
that would sweep that area. We had arrived the night
before and spent the night in a local hotel. The next
morning the pastor came to the hotel and gave us the
news that he was going to have to cancel the meeting
because of the rising flood waters. I felt that I didn't
want to leave the town until I had gone to the pastor's
house to pray for its protection. "The water is already
within thirty feet of the house," he said, "but one of
the brothers will take you there."

I went back to our room to tell the other ladies who
had come with us what was happening, and when I
got there they told me that I had received a phone
call while I was out. It was from a lady in the north-
ern part of Minnesota. She had been watching the
news of the worsening flood in Fargo. When I called
her back, she said, "We were planning on coming to
the convention, but I understand now that it's been
canceled. Since you're not going to be ministering in
Fargo, would you mind coming to a little place in
Minnesota?"

"Where are you?" I asked.

"We're in Milaca," she said. "I haven't had time to
talk to the pastor yet, but I think he would be willing

to have you, if you're willing to come. If we can't arrange a meeting at the church, we'll find some other place to have it."

We would have to catch a flight out to Minneapolis and get there in time to drive to Milaca. We told her we would do our best to arrange it, and we quickly got our things together to leave for the airport, promising to call her when we knew out flight number and arrival time.

Before we left Fargo, we went by the pastor's house to believe God for a miracle. Many young people were there sandbagging the property and, as the pastor had told us, the water was now only thirty feet away. I began to sing in the Spirit and to speak to the flood. As we left that day, I had the assurance that the flood waters would not overflow their house. Later the pastor's wife called us to say that theirs was the only house in the area that had not suffered severe damage from the flood. God had given them a great miracle.

We were able to get to the Fargo Airport and take a flight to Minneapolis. The sister from Milaca met us and took us directly to her town for the evening service in her church. Some of the people who attended had come from a great distance, driving as much as ten hours to get there. Some of them were from South Dakota and had been planning to attend the meetings in Fargo. Having learned about the cancellation, they drove all the way to Milaca instead.

I found it very interesting that the associate pastor of the church, Brother John, had said to the pastor just a few days before, "One day, Sister Ruth is going to be here in our church." The pastor had thought that was improbable, but here we were. John felt very honored that God had given him that knowing in his spirit. Because the meetings in Fargo were canceled, God had brought me to their church.

One night during those meetings, I was telling the people about being in Malaysia the previous June and that I was going back there the following June. I felt that the pastor from Milaca, Minnesota, should go to Malacca, Malaysia and minister (the two names, Milaca and Malacca, are pronounced the same). He did go, and the trip opened up a whole new aspect of ministry for him.

Stop struggling with your ministry schedule and let God make it for you. He wills excellence for your life, not only in the spiritual, but also in the natural. He has called us to an *"excelling glory"*:

> *For even that which was made glorious had no glory in this respect, by reason of the glory that excelleth.* 2 Corinthians 3:10

You can excel in the day-by-day operation of your business in the glory. God wants you to do well with the activities of your life. In fact, He wants you to excel to the honor of the Lord. May men know that it is because He is going before you and searching out the place of excellence for you.

Some of us get nervous if things happen too suddenly and too easily. We think it should take so much struggle and suffering that when God does it easily, we feel uncomfortable. When God puts the person we need right in our pathway, we wonder if it's a trick of some kind.

You might need a plumber, for example. You can go looking through the yellow pages and hope that you are calling someone who is honest and capable. Or you can let God put the right person beside you on the bus and let them speak to you. Don't be surprised when the man next to you says, "I'm a plumber." God is going before you, and He is preparing the way.

Can we not trust the Spirit of God? Can we not know that He is working out all the details of our lives? Can we not know that He is taking away all the struggles of life and smoothing the way for us? Start excelling unto the honor of God through the ease of the glory realm.

I have such confidence about the days just ahead of us and am convinced that, for those of us who desire to accomplish the fullness of what God has for us, it will come without us having to struggle for it. Dramatic changes are coming, but I am not distressed over them. I refuse to become anxious because God is on my side. While I am sitting in His presence, He is

searching. While I am meditating on Him, He is working on my behalf.

I have determined not to be too quick to leave the
presence of the Lord, as I see some doing. Sometimes
our services get better and better as they go along,
and some people have left just when the best things
are beginning to happen. I want to wait in the Lord's
presence until He has determined my future for me.

God's glory covers us. He is over every affair of our
daily existence and is bringing us into a fuller realm
than we have ever imagined.

I love the searchings and researchings of God. He
knows what He is doing. If I am considering God, He
is so vast and great that I wouldn't even know what
subject to begin with. Where do I start?

Thank God that He knows more than the ABCs. He
also knows the XYZs. When I allow the Spirit of God
to search out the secret places of my life, when I take
time to sit down under His tree and allow His fruit to
be sweet to my taste, I am never disappointed.

Jacob didn't know how to search out the things of
God for his life, but when he rested his head on that
stone that became his pillow, suddenly a stairway
between Earth and Heaven appeared above his head,
and he saw the angels of God ascending and descend-
ing on it. I want to experience that same thing over
and over. I want to go to bed at night and see Heaven
opened above my head.

I know that we live in a natural world, and most

people want us to constantly be considering the natural. But when we refuse to be dragged down by the circumstances of our lives and, instead, concentrate on the heavenly, one by one the natural things of our lives will fall into place and submit themselves to God's order. I want every step of my life to be ordered by God. I want every contact I make to be ordered by God. I want every person with whom I interact to be ordered by God.

God is putting your life together, and if you will live under His glory cloud you will not have one misstep. Everyone who crosses your pathway will be part of God's greater plan for your excellence: for your city, for your country, for your family, and for your ministry.

Your ministry should not be a constant struggle. God wants to take charge of it and guide it to excellence in His glory. *His glory is rest, and His rest is the glory.*

In the natural sense, there is very little rest for those who are involved in revival. So much is happening, and it is happening so quickly. There are many open doors, many invitations, many opportunities. And this will only increase. The only rest we will know in these end times will be the rest in the glory of the Lord. And if we are not covered in the glory, we will not know any rest at all.

The Lord has so much to say to us, so much to teach us. He longs to teach us by His Spirit and for men to recognize what He has done by saying, "Those are taught of the Lord." He wants to make clear to us all the things we have been longing to comprehend, and He wants to do it with such ease that there is no struggle at all. He wants to satisfy the deep hunger within us.

Our Heavenly Father,

Take the struggles from our lives. Let Your cloud of glory move and help us to move with it. Go before us and search out a resting place for us, in ministry, in Your divine purposes in every sense. We yield to Your will and give You complete authority to plan our lives in every detail. We will follow after You and live under the cloud of Your glory.

Teach us what we need to know by Your Spirit in order to bring forth excellence in our lives.

In Jesus' name,
Amen!

Chapter 14

Avoiding What Hinders the Glory

And grieve not the holy Spirit of God, whereby ye are sealed unto the day of redemption.
                                        Ephesians 4:30

Quench not the Spirit.   1 Thessalonians 5:19

The next summer after the Indian couple received that great financial miracle, the husband was at the summer campmeeting again, and this time he began to flow in wonderful revelation. At various points in the service, he saw angels at work, saw sparks of fire emanating from someone as they praised or saw the cloud of God's glory hovering over an individual or over the congregation as they worshiped.

I said to him, "Brother, would you do me a favor? I'm learning more and more how to respond to the glory, how to bring the glory in, and what enhances the glory. I have learned that some things don't, so we let them go. When you see these things that God is showing you, would you make a note of what I'm saying or doing or what's happening in the service at the time of the manifestation of the glory or the visi-

tation of the angels so that I can go back later and re-
view them and see what is working for us or what
we need to let go of as we minister?" He graciously
agreed and that summer kept a little *glory notebook* for
us, from which we learned so much.

Sometimes we said the wrong things, and the glory
would begin to fade. When we found that fact noted,
we knew that we didn't want to say those things anymore. At other times we would say something that
would cause sparks to fly in every direction. And,
once that fact was noticed, we knew that we wanted
to say those things more and more.

One thing that can hinder the flow of the glory of
God in our midst is our unwillingness to love one
another as Jesus loved us. In the moments of my greatest frustration with people, God's Spirit has whispered
to my heart and said, "This is one for whom Christ
died." When this has happened, my heart has suddenly been melted, for no matter what I thought, if
the Lord died for that person, who was I to say anything against them? Who was I to lift up my voice
against them? Who was I to be frustrated or agitated
or exasperated with them? Who was I to feel like I
have come to the end of my rope with that person? I
must forgive and flow in forgiveness.

Forgiveness is so powerful that, in that moment,
thinking of the fact that Christ died for that person, I
found that I had forgotten what it was that made me

frustrated with them in the first place. Forgiveness can keep you sane. It keeps you anointed.

A pastor coming to the camp from Pakistan spoke to my brother. "Don't believe every pastor when he comes from our country and says that he has been preaching to multitudes. In general, it is not so. It happened to me only after I began to watch carefully what I heard and what I said. The care I exercised in those two areas brought a new flow of miracles to my life, and only then did I begin to preach to multitudes."

Recently Barbara Lanzdorf had a vision of ministers standing behind the pulpit preaching. Out of one side of the mouths flowed a stream of locusts that ate up the harvest. Criticism, bitterness, backbiting, and strife will eat up the very harvest you are believing for.

One touch of God's glory melts the hardest heart. It causes *"the mountains [to] flow down to the sea."* Let even the little hills in your spirit be removed. When the glory of God is moving, even a dark shadow of thought that shouldn't be there can hinder you. Get rid of it, and let the Spirit of God humble you.

Over a period of time we have learned that some of the things which most adversely affect the flow of the glory of God in our midst are these:

- Our desire to please people
- Our fear of appearing too simple, too unlearned

- Our inability to count all our knowledge as dung, as Paul did
- Our desire to impress people with our education, skills and abilities and with who we are
- Our inability to unlearn what we have already learned when God is attempting to lead us into new things
- Our inability or unwillingness to lay aside tradition
- Our unwillingness to forgive others

God wants to give us all a greater sensitivity in this regard. If we can learn to know the cloud — whether there are five people present or fifty or five hundred or five thousand or fifty thousand — we will be able to stand under the cloud and minister directly from the glory unto the people. *This is revival glory.*

We may well have to throw out some of the old in order to obtain the new, but the Lord will help us and teach us. He has promised to be our Instructor. He has promised to lead us forth, and He will — if we are determined to stand under the glory cloud or to stand in it.

When you discover things that seem to contribute to the glory, do those things more; and when you find things that seem to diminish the glory, stop doing them. It's as simple as that.

There's a certain harshness that has become "Pentecostal style," an approach that has come to be accepted as the manner of the prophet who wants to "call down fire" from Heaven. The only problem is that those who adopt this style are calling fire down on the saints and not the false prophets. They forget that Jesus is the greatest example of the prophet, and that He demonstrated a gentle spirit. Don't hesitate to move into the gentleness of the glory.

Some may accuse us of having just one thing that we harp on constantly, but if that one thing brings the glory, let's do it — whatever people say. Let's sing the notes we know until God teaches us more notes. Be faithful to sing the two notes you know until God gives you notes three, four and five. Do whatever you have to do to move into the eternal realm. And when we learn the things that quench the Spirit and grieve the heart of the Spirit of God so that He withdraws, let us willingly and joyfully abandon those things that we might move ever upward into the greater glory He has prepared for us.

I have found that singing in the Spirit is one of the easiest ways of coming into the glory and remaining there.

Lord,

Take from us those things that detract from the glory, and add to us those things that increase it.

For Your name's sake,
Amen!

Chapter 15

Maintaining the Simplicity of the Glory

This is the word of the LORD unto Zerubbabel,
saying, Not by might, nor by power, but by my
spirit, saith the LORD of hosts.   Zechariah 4:6

Zechariah's vision was a complicated one, but God's message for Zerubbabel was simple, and that same simple message is for every generation: *NOT BY MIGHT, NOR BY POWER, BUT BY MY SPIRIT, SAITH THE LORD OF HOSTS.*

I find that God is continually bringing us back and reminding us of this truth — over and over again. It is one of the most quoted verses in Spirit-filled circles. We know it, and we repeat it often. In the midst of the complexity of our lives, God still has to remind us. We are adding so much to our lives that He wants us to know, again, that there is nothing we can do that will bring us victory. Victory only comes by what He does in us and through us.

When my book *Glory* was first published, many of the songs were handwritten. Some thought that made the book look "homemade," and they didn't take it very seriously. When they got around to reading the book, however, they found in it what they had been looking for.

Several people told me that *Glory* was actually in their houses untouched and unread. When they continued to ask the Lord for the answer for revival, He told them that He had already sent them the answer and that they needed to read the book.

In later versions, the songs were more professionally done, but I think there was a purpose in having them very simply done in the first place. We can get so talented, so professional and polished that we can't relax and allow God to do the work by His Spirit. It is even possible for us to get so full of the "Word" that we can't seem to let go and let God do His work through the simplicity of the Spirit that is so profound.

My friend David Du Plessis, the great South African apostle to America and the world, continually confounded theologians and great minds all across denominational lines by his profound simplicity. Our abilities, our knowledge and our experiences sometimes limit us from receiving the greater things that God wants to do for us. We just get too complicated.

Tell me, which church choir would condescend to sing the song of the angels, *Holy, Holy, Holy*, and which choir director would allow them to sing it?

When many of those songs were given to us in Jerusalem, we didn't have trained musicians to do the musical notation, but that limitation proved to be to our advantage. If we had been better trained, we might have rejected the simplicity of the choruses in the first place.

The simplicity of a thing is important. This is the reason God has to continually raise up new movements. When the former movement gets so sophisticated and polished that it loses its ability to move out into the flow of new things that God is doing, He is forced to move on. It is possible to get TOO organized. Anytime we get to the place that our dependence on the Holy Ghost is limited, He goes elsewhere.

In many circles, people can preach whether the Holy Spirit is present or not, and, most of the time, they do. When the message is finished, we can all say, "What a great sermon," but few of us can say, "What great glory! What a fresh touch of the Spirit upon the people!"

I prefer it when I hear people operating in the Spirit who don't seem polished. When I know that they are reaching for the next word, I know that what is coming is from God.

There are exceptions to this principle. Some very polished vessels still maintain the ability to be childlike in their response to God. The best example I know of this is my dear friend Monsignor Walsh of Wynnewood, Pennsylvania.

Others take the opposite approach. "You know that can't be from God," they say. "That person stuttered and stumbled." But sometimes the stutter and the

stumble proves more than anything to me that it WAS
God.

On the Day of Pentecost, God showed us that He
works through imperfect men. Peter, who only a few
day before had denied the Lord, was the one used on
that day to bless so many. His experience in the Upper Room changed his life forever. Three thousand
were added to the Church that first day and another
five thousand a few days later. We can trust the Holy
Spirit and know that what He does will be done well.

> *And the angel that talked with me came again,*
> *and waked me, as a man that is wakened out of*
> *his sleep.*   Zechariah 4:1

The angel woke up the prophet, although he was
apparently already awake. He said he was *"as a man*
that is wakened out of his sleep." He was awake, yet the
angel woke him up. I know a lot of people like that.
They seem to be awake, but they surely need to be
awakened in the Spirit. God wants us to be WIDE
awake in this revival.

The angel spoke with Zechariah:

> *And said unto me, What seest thou? And I said,*
> *I have looked, and behold a candlestick all of gold,*
> *with a bowl upon the top of it, and his seven lamps*
> *thereon, and seven pipes to the seven lamps,*
> *which are upon the top thereof: And two olive*

*trees by it, one upon the right side of the bowl,
and the other upon the left side thereof. So I answered and spake to the angel that talked with
me, saying, What are these, my lord? Then the
angel that talked with me answered and said unto
me, Knowest thou not what these be? And I said,
No, my lord. Then he answered and spake unto
me, saying, This is the word of the* LORD *unto
Zerubbabel, saying, Not by might, nor by power,
but by my spirit, saith the* LORD *of hosts.*

Zechariah 4:2-6

*Who art thou, O great mountain? before
Zerubbabel thou shalt become a plain: and he shall
bring forth the headstone thereof with shoutings,
crying, Grace, grace unto it. Moreover the word
of the* LORD *came unto me, saying, The hands of
Zerubbabel have laid the foundation of this house;
his hands shall also finish it; and thou shalt know
that the* LORD *of hosts hath sent me unto you.
For who hath despised the day of small things?
for they shall rejoice, and shall see the plummet
in the hand of Zerubbabel with those seven; they
are the eyes of the* LORD, *which run to and fro
through the whole earth. Then answered I, and
said unto him, What are these two olive trees
upon the right side of the candlestick and upon
the left side thereof? And I answered again, and
said unto him, What be these two olive branches*

which through the two golden pipes empty the
golden oil out of themselves? And he answered
me and said, Knowest thou not what these be?
And I said, No, my lord. Then said he, These are
the two anointed ones, that stand by the Lord of
the whole earth.   Zechariah 4:7-14

Zerubbabel was given the message that the hands
which had laid the foundations of the house would
be the same hands that would see the completion. God
finishes what He begins. And if God has given you a
beginning, He will anoint you to finish the work. The
same anointing it takes to start something is the same
anointing it takes to finish it. As the writer to the Hebrews said:

Looking unto Jesus the author and finisher of our
faith ...   Hebrews 12:2

If you need miracles to get a thing going, you will
need miracles to get it finished.

These great candelabra had a source of oil, and the
two who stood beside the pipes that supplied the oil
were the sons of oil, or the oily ones. Never be
ashamed of the anointing. You can arrive somewhere
with nothing else, but don't arrive without the anointing. If you lose your suitcase, you will live without it,
but don't try to live without the anointing.

I travel so much that once my luggage was lost several times in one week. I never blame the airlines. God is in control of my life, and sometimes He wants to teach us something. One lesson I have learned is that God doesn't want us to be dependent on whatever we happen to be carrying in that suitcase. One summer I had to buy a new Bible every few weeks, when I arrived somewhere to preach and didn't even have a Bible to read. Sometimes there was no time or opportunity to buy a new Bible, and I was forced to preach from the treasures within me. I discovered that I have enough to preach. God has invested His riches into my life.

When I go to bed at night, I hear the Word of God reverberating in my soul, and when I awaken to start a new day, it is there fresh and new for that day too. God's treasure is within me. When you discover enough treasures within your own life, you are no longer dependent upon a suitcase.

When you come into a church service, people should never know that you have just learned of some personal tragedy in your life two minutes before you entered. Rather they should experience the treasure that is in you.

As I taught in my book *Glory*, we often get much too complicated in our worship services, and the result can be tragic. If the songs are not simple enough, we are unable to flow together. Personally, I feel robbed in such services. When I am not being given the opportunity to worship the Lord with everyone else, I miss what I came for in the first place. I go to the House of God to meet God, to touch His glory, and I'm not satisfied unless I do. Since God uses praising and worshiping to bring in the glory, when the congregation is not given the privilege to worship, we all feel robbed and may go home feeling frustrated. It is wrong for those leading the service to get so complicated that they deny others the opportunity and the privilege of moving into the simple flow of the Spirit of God by praising and worshiping.

Recently, I was at a meeting where the song leader wanted to let us all know how many new songs he had learned. I thought maybe the young people would know the songs he was singing. Although I personally know thousands of choruses, I didn't know one of these. I looked around to see if I was right, if maybe this was a generational thing, but none of the young people were singing either. Out of the whole congregation of several hundred people, there were only a few people singing with the worship leader. Finally, I stepped up to him and whispered in his ear, "Sing something that we all know so that we can all sing and be blessed."

It's fine for the song leader to close his eyes and worship God as he sings, but there are times when we need to open our eyes and see if anybody else is singing with us. If they are not, we need to shift into something that everyone can sing. Even if it's not the latest chorus, and even if it's not the particular rhythm in which we want to sing, it is better to sing something that the congregation knows so that they can flow with us to the goodness of the Lord.

It takes the same consecration to live in the glory as it does to experience it in the first place. One night, Sister Ruth Carneal was leading our campmeeting service, and the Lord spoke to her and gave her a little new song, telling her that those who would sing it would be delivered from sadness, sorrow and heaviness of heart. It actually sounded more like a drum beat than it did a melody. She thought to herself, "I don't do those funny little sounds like some people do," and she resisted. When the Lord continued to impress upon her this simple drum beat, "bum-bum, ba ba bum," she finally did it, and everyone joined her.

The next day a brother from Uganda who was staying on the campground and attending the meetings came to her and said, "Yesterday, I got word that my mother had died in Uganda. All day I experienced a great sadness. I was sad not only that she had died and I was not there, but also that I would not be able to go home for her funeral. But when you began to do the African drumbeat song, and I began to sing it, God instantly delivered me from my sorrow and sadness." He told that story several times in the coming days. He was not only delivered from his sadness; he was totally delivered.

In everything we do, we must retain the simplicity of the glory and let God be God in our lives.

Lord,

Help us to maintain simplicity before You, always relying on You and You alone.

In Jesus' name,
Amen!

Chapter 16

Letting the Glory Flow

He that believeth on me, as the scripture hath said,
out of his belly shall flow rivers of living water.
(But this spake he of the Spirit, which they that
believe on him should receive.)   John 7:38-39

Learn to relax in God's presence so that you can be
carried by the flow of His river. You can't release the
flow; only He can, so let Him do it. Let Him bring
you forth into an ease. You can't carry His river, but
His river can carry you. Be carried away by the Spirit
again and again. Let Him bring you forth into the fullness of this new day. He will do it for you — if you
will just yield to Him.

When we were children and played Pin the Tail on
the Donkey, they put a blindfold on us and turned us
around a couple of times so that we were disoriented
and had to figure out which way we were going. And
that's what God has to do with some of us. He has to
spin us around a bit until we lose our sense of direction and are willing to just relax in His arms and let
Him carry us where He will. It seems a shame to have
to lose our sense of direction in order to find our way,

but some people can't do it any other way. If we don't learn to flow with the new, we'll be just like everyone else.

It isn't hard to have a vision. It isn't hard to see Jesus. You just have to learn to relax in the Spirit. That's when it happens, when you stop struggling and start relaxing and being carried away by the stream of God's glory.

There is no greater key word for our times than the word "flow." That's the secret of receiving God's best in this hour. Get in the flow, and flow with God. In every service where we get in the flow, the anointing comes in fuller measure. When we have a lot of stops and starts, we can never achieve the same heights of glory. Praise is important and worship is important, but if you don't get into the flow of the Spirit as you are praising and worshiping, the glory will not come.

It doesn't take great ability to flow with the river. Just stop resisting, and it will carry you. Just relax and let God have His way, and He will do the work. Lay aside your reasoning. Lay aside your understanding. Lay aside all the other stumbling blocks, and you will find yourself being swept along with the current of the Spirit.

As the river flows, revelation flows. As the river flows, vision flows. As the river flows, miracles flow. As the river flows, there is healing and deliverance and victory.

When we begin to flow with the river, we may have

no idea where that flow is taking us. If we need to know, the Lord will tell us, but usually we don't need to know. Just get with the flow and, as you flow, God will drop the vision into your spirit and prepare you for where the river is taking you. It will sometimes be to an individual, other times to a church or congregation or perhaps to a city, state, or nation. He may even carry you out into the realms of the heavenlies.

Sometimes in order to get into the flow of the glory you must forget your prayer list. Don't worry about it. God will put His thoughts into your spirit. He will bring to your remembrance the things you need to speak with Him about, and if He doesn't remind you of something, you had best forget it. He knows what is important at the moment.

He reminds me of people I haven't seen in years. Nothing has happened that would cause me to remember them, to think about them, to be burdened for them, yet God puts them into my spirit while I'm flowing in His river. God brings people before me that I have met at some point in my life. I have long ago forgotten their names, but He shows me their faces. He even brings their names to my remembrance — if it is important. It happens in the flow.

We are in the river, and the river is in us. We stand in it, and it flows through us. Let the river flow. That's the whole message of the revival. "Let" means "allow or permit." Stop preventing it. Let it happen. Stop sidestepping the water. Let the river flow where it will, and get into the flow yourself.

Let all the dams be removed. Let the river do what it was designed to do. Remove any obstacle to its flow.

Most of us would never think of consciously quenching the Spirit; but, at the same time, most of us are not willing to let the river flow. Stop quenching it. Stop preventing it. Stop avoiding it. Let it flow.

Stop frustrating God's purposes. He wants to flood your soul with blessing. Why do we not trust Him? His river has one purpose and that is to give life. Ezekiel declared it:

> *And every thing shall live whither the river cometh.*   Ezekiel 47:9

Every time Jesus spoke of water, He spoke of life. This is water of life. This is a river of life:

> *And whosoever will, let him take of the water of life freely.*   Revelation 22:17

Wherever this river goes, nothing can stay dead. Everything in its path receives life. And the more we allow the river of God to flow through us the less of death will be found in us. We all have a little death that works in us from time to time, sometimes more than at other times, but God is causing that death to be washed away from our lives by the flow of His river. Be so touched by the river that anyone you touch will know life, that whatever situation you move in, you can bring life to it.

The river will keep you young and vibrant. It will keep you full and excited. It will keep you in health and strength.

When the river of God is released in our lives, it flows out through other tongues. When you speak in tongues, you are participating in the river. You are letting the river flow through you. God has chosen to let the river come out of us. Through praising and worship Him, we give the river an opportunity to flow.

David said:

> *To the end that my glory may sing praise to thee, and not be silent. O LORD my God, I will give thanks unto thee for ever.* Psalm 30:12

He called his tongue his glory, showing that the glory of God takes over our tongues and uses them for His purposes. Let the river flow through you, out of your innermost being and out of your tongue.

God is looking for yielded tongues. When someone yields to the Holy Spirit and gives Him a voice, He can do amazing things in our midst. When John heard the voices of those who were gathered before the throne of God, it sounded to him like *"many waters."*

That shows me that those voices were connected with the river. Let it be my voice, Lord.

Ezekiel identified the believer with that heavenly sound. That doesn't mean that you necessarily sing well. It means that you are in contact with the river and that the river is flowing through you.

A man called me from Atlanta, Georgia to ask what weekends I would be at the camp here in Ashland, Virginia, and as I spoke with him, I could hear the sound of glory in his voice. He was in contact with the river. I didn't know him at all, and we were not talking about spiritual matters. We were talking about schedules. But I heard enough over the telephone line that I could have told you a lot about the man. Later I asked and learned that he had been a missionary to Russia and Bulgaria. But I already knew that he was a man who had touched the glory.

My friend Marcus Lamb, owner of Channel 29 in Dallas, Channel 41 in Denver and Channel 32 in Macon, Georgia, likewise has the sound of glory in his voice. Sister Ruth Carneal, one of our associate pastors here, has a singing voice that carries the sound of glory. The time will come that the whole Bride of Christ will have a voice like this, with the sound of glory on it, *"the sound of many waters."*

The river is not only with us wherever we happen to be at the moment, but it is in us, and when we speak, that river can be heard in the sound of our voices. Ezekiel said:

> *And when they went, I heard the noise of their*
> *wings, like the noise of great waters, as the voice*
> *of the Almighty, the voice of speech, as the noise*
> *of an host: when they stood, they let down their*
> *wings. And there was a voice from the firmament*
> *that was over their heads, when they stood, and*
> *had let down their wings.*   Ezekiel 1:24-25

In Hebrew this word *voice* is the same as the word *sound*. Ezekiel was hearing *"the sound of the Almighty"* coming forth from the living creatures. So *"the sound of God's voice"* is *"as the noise of great waters."* The descriptive phrase that speaks of God's voice becomes the descriptive phrase that speaks of the voice of the Bride of Christ. Whether we are speaking a word of prophecy, giving forth a word of knowledge, or just asking God for guidance, we can speak forth the glory of the Lord with our lips. Let the river flow.

Get into this move of the Holy Ghost. The enemy will try every way he can to paralyze you so that you cannot be moved by the Spirit. But if you will resist everything that he tries to do, you will be victorious. Resist him in the name of the Lord. Say to the enemy, "I am determined to be moved by the Spirit of God. You cannot hold me back."

One of the reasons God is sending so many of His people to the floor under the anointing of men and women of faith is that He wants us to remain ready and willing to yield to the Holy Ghost at all times. We can get out of the habit and actually forget how to yield to Him.

You might ask, "Sister Ruth, do we have to go down on the floor?" No, but there's enough power available for you to go down. So if you don't, you're probably not yielding to the Spirit of God when a man or woman of God lays hands on you.

For many years I didn't often pray for people individually in my meetings. I led everyone together to the throne of God. I recognize that the laying on of hands and the accompanying manifestations are signs God has given of His power being demonstrated in this day.

It's not by the will of men. It's being moved by the Holy Ghost. God's teaching us more and more how to yield.

The songs that we sing now about the river and its flow are different from the ones we sang twenty years ago, for in each revival there comes a different emphasis. But it is the same river that is flowing in our midst.

We need to draw on the heavenly dimension and let it flow into us and then flow out of us. Flow! That's the key word of the revival. It doesn't matter how great the river is. If you don't let it flow, its waters become dead, and all blessing ceases. You don't need a new Dead Sea in your life. You need a river of life, and it must be allowed to flow.

In connection with flow, there is another word that we must learn and be aware of. It is the word SPONTANEOUS. God is calling us to allow Him to work spontaneously in our midst. When we first get started in the prophetic realm, the exercise of the supernatural gifts of God, He often permits certain things. Later, He will not permit those same things, and it is because the giftings of God must be spontaneous.

When we first started worshiping on Mt. Zion in St. Peter in Gallicantu Church, our group of twenty-five young people would gather early before each service to praise the Lord. Seven o'clock in the evening was too early for both the local people and the visiting tourists to come, but since we were borrowing the church and had to be out of the building by nine o'clock each night, we took advantage of that extra time to seek the Lord. We called it our "warm-up" time. Others could join us if they wanted, but we wanted that extra time with the Lord.

Sister Janet Saunders who lived and worked with us for many years in Jerusalem later had one of the great prophetic giftings, and in that thirty minute interval, from seven to seven-thirty each evening, God would give her a little vision or a little revelation. Sometime between seven-thirty and nine, she would step up and prophesy. What she said would be a fuller understanding of what God had revealed to her between seven and seven-thirty. What God had shown her in the warm-up session was just a foretaste to give her boldness to step up in the service later and let the fullness of the river flow.

After a few months, I said to her one day, "From now on, don't try to reach into the Spirit before the main service to get a foretaste of what God wants to say. When you stand in the main service and prophesy, I want it to be without any forethought at all." Every gift of the Spirit should be as speaking in tongues is, totally spontaneous.

God is causing His excellence to come forth in us. Not only is the cream rising to the top, but you can make butter from it. Normally, all the bad of our lives floats to the top and has to be scooped off, but now it is time for all the good to rise, the excellence of the Spirit to dominate.

Most of us are already flowing in the things of the Spirit, but what God wants is more and more spontaneity. The great things that God will do in this hour will not require forethought on our part. The wind of the Spirit will come in and we will have to respond to it that very moment, without having prepared ourselves in any way, other than being in the Spirit.

When God gives us a full sentence of what He wants to say through us in prophecy so that we will have courage to stand up and give the rest, self tries to get into the picture and improve on the sentence God is giving us. God doesn't say things like we might say them on our own. When the spontaneous flow comes we sometimes don't know what we have said or why we have said it.

A few months ago in our Richmond church one Sunday night there was a wonderful prophetic flow in the service. I whispered to the person in charge of the service to keep it flowing. Pastors have the authority and the ability to channel the flow of what is happening, to stop it, or to encourage it. Sometimes we feel obligated to visiting speakers to give them extra time, but that night we had nothing to restrain us.

The resulting flow of the Spirit was so exquisite that I count it as one of the great nights of my life. I saw the river of God pouring out of people's lips, and I knew that the source of the river on the Earth is the mouths of the believers. One after another, humble people moved forward to describe what God was showing them, what God was giving them, what God was saying to them. Wonderful revelation came forth.

Some saw the rainbow of glory coming out of the mouths of people in the river. I saw the seven lamps of fire that burn before the throne flowing out of people's mouths in the river. Every aspect of God that you could think about was flowing out of the mouths of the people in revelation knowledge.

Everything that He is is in the river. He is the river. This is one of the ways He manifests Himself. When the river bubbles up within us, it is God moving in the depths of our souls, and when His revelation begins to flow forth from our mouths, it is God speaking to us and through us.

This phrase *"living water"* means "flowing water." Jewish people will never be baptized in water that is not *"chai,"* alive, and that means moving, flowing. In our experience, there must be an intake and there must be an outlet. There must be a flow in, and there must be a flow out. Jesus is the living water, and He wants to flow in us and through us.

With the flow of the river comes the revelation of God. When a small child sees something, he or she often cannot describe it fully as an adult might. An artistic or poetic person may be able to describe what they see much more fully than the rest of us. But in the river, it is according to our ability to yield to God, not according to our life's experience or our life's education that we are able to describe what we see.

You don't need to do a computer search. Just open your mouth and let the river flow, God working in us and through us, showing us these things.

One night in Dallas, after doing a television program, we were invited to a home for fellowship. There I was asked to pray a blessing over a certain brother. When I put my hand on him, I could sense that he was a good brother. Then, suddenly, I experienced something for the first time in my life. I felt the great waves of the river moving up and down his back, although he was not physically moving. When I opened my eyes after a few moments, he was a totally new man. You may feel some of it in an external sense, but the great bulk of it will impact your spirit.

Oh, I urge you, let the river flow. Let God change you too.

Lord,

Cause us to flow like a mighty river. Bring forth the ease of flowing.

In Jesus' name,
Amen!

Chapter 17

Flowing Together in the Glory

Hear the word of the Lord, O ye nations, and declare it in the isles afar off, and say, He that scattered Israel will gather him, and keep him, as a shepherd doth his flock. For the Lord hath redeemed Jacob, and ransomed him from the hand of him that was stronger than he. Therefore they shall come and sing in the height of Zion, and shall flow together to the goodness of the Lord, for wheat, and for wine, and for oil, and for the young of the flock and of the herd: and their soul shall be as a watered garden; and they shall not sorrow any more at all. Then shall the virgin rejoice in the dance, both young men and old together: for I will turn their mourning into joy, and will comfort them, and make them rejoice from their sorrow. And I will satiate the soul of the priests with fatness, and my people shall be satisfied with my goodness, saith the Lord.

Jeremiah 31:10-14

If we want the wheat, the wine and the oil, we must learn not only how to flow but how to flow together.

Flowing is individual, and flowing together is congregational. This is the reason praise and worship is being restored in the congregation. Many of the things that are happening to us as congregations used to happen to us as we worshiped alone in our homes. When we first went to Israel, one of the things that amazed people was that we were doing *"in the midst of the congregation"* what they only did privately at home. God is bringing the simplicity of the "home prayer meeting" into the main sanctuary during Sunday morning worship service.

God is teaching us how to flow together. We are becoming a congregation, not just in symbol, but "the congregation of the Lord." That word congregation just means "those who gather." And we are gathering unto the Lord in these days and learning how to flow together in His glory.

That's why we should do many things together. We should stand together; we should lift up our voices together; we should raise our hands together; and we should dance together. At first, it may be a mechanical lifting up, but as we obey the Lord in this act of unity, before long we will feel the moving of the river of God and know that we are one in Him.

We may begin worshiping as many voices, but when He does the miracle in us, those many voices become one voice. As we join together at the feet of Jesus, we must each lay aside his or her individual agenda, so that we can all find His agenda and begin to flow together to the goodness of the Lord unto the harvest of wheat and wine and oil.

Wheat and wine and oil were products of the crops that typically were grown around Jerusalem and Judea. The most common tithe, therefore, that was brought unto the House of God, was one or more of these three items. Sometimes the harvest was better than at other times, and the resulting tithe brought up to Jerusalem would be more abundant than at other times. We are on the brink of the greatest harvest the world has ever seen, and the blessing which will be gathered in will outstrip anything we have seen or heard of until now.

If you want to flow in God, you have to participate in what He is doing. When I'm in Africa and the people are dancing, I jump up and dance with them, attempting to dance more or less as they do, although perhaps I have never danced in exactly that way before. I may not do it very well, but I do it with all my heart and do not hinder their flow by trying to introduce my American style.

Lay aside your preconceived ideas, and learn to flow with what God is doing. Join those who are leading the service and get in the flow of what they are doing. Unity is powerful. This is not the day for individualism and independence. Don't be stubborn and lock yourself out of the move of God. Independence will rob you of the blessing. Get into the flow and learn to move with the river — flowing together.

The glory of God is only revealed in its fullness when we are together. There were only a few times when Moses did something independently of the other children of Israel. For the most part, they did things together. They camped together, and they rose up together to move on. Flow has nothing to do with "I did it my way" or "I've got to be me." You flow with Brother Jones in the service today, and he will flow with you in the service tomorrow.

Yes, Moses, as the leader of the people, went alone to the top of the mountain and stood in the cloud of God's glory. Most of the time, however, Moses was right there with the people, and God is dealing with ministers to reach out in a congregational sense to see what God will do for the people as a whole. You and I must learn more and more to respond to the Holy Ghost in others and with others.

I love services where many people jump up and prophesy. We would see it more often, but some don't yield to their gift. When it does happen, one person sees the river of God, the next person sees where the river of God is heading, the third person sees what is happening in the river, and still another sees what the river will do next. I love it. I love it. I love it. And I am convinced that God loves it, too.

Some people have great notebooks filled with teachings of every kind, but have never learned how to flow with what they have been taught. When our people were learning Hebrew at the *Ulpans* in Israel, we all had wonderful notebooks. I told the others, "You may have a wonderful notebook; you may have recorded well what the teacher said; but if you can't speak it, you didn't learn anything." Speaking Hebrew is the whole purpose of attending an *Ulpan*. It is not for the purpose of developing wonderful notebooks. It is the same way in the Spirit. It is time to lay aside the notebooks and start doing what the Lord is teaching us, flowing together in the river of God.

One year, in Jerusalem, when we were having an around-the-clock prayer meeting for the ten days leading up to Pentecost, late one night a young brother began to have a revelation and to sing: "We are gathering the pearls and flinging them to the gates of glory." As we got absorbed in the flow of what he was seeing, we realized that God was speaking to us about the opening of China. I dropped everything in Jerusalem and, the next day, flew off to Hong Kong to do an intensive study of Mandarin, not knowing how God would open that seemingly impenetrable door, but knowing that He would do it if I obeyed Him. It was nearly impossible for the average American to even visit China in those days. These were the days before normalization, and the only way to get in was to be invited by a resident foreign diplomat. God knew that too.

I miraculously found an excellent tutor and, the next day, sitting in her house at lunchtime was startled to hear her niece say that she was the wife of an Australian diplomat stationed in Beijing and that they would be happy to facilitate the invitation I needed to get in. On the second day that I was obeying the Lord by sitting to learn the language, He opened the door for me to go into China. It was the beginning of flinging the pearls toward the gates of glory and had all come about because of our flowing together in the Spirit. If you can only learn to flow together in the Spirit amazing things will happen for you as well.

It is far too competitive in the ministry. We must learn to flow together. We are all on the same team. I have to ask the Lord to give me grace to endure sometimes when I see preachers in a conference, each one trying to out-preach the other. This is not a competition. Forget your individual identification and start flowing together unto the goodness of the Lord.

I know that some people think it will never happen, but it's coming. If God can bring the Jewish people from the north, the south, the east and the west and form of them a great nation, He can certainly get us gentile Christians together. The unity which the Jewish people see in us will stir them to jealousy and cause them to cry out to God in a fuller manner. God can do it for us.

One April, in the pastors conference in Brownsville, Florida, someone started a Jericho March. One by one everyone joined in, as we flowed together to the glory of God. We didn't need a personal invitation, and no one needed to beckon to us to join. Spontaneously each one took his place in the procession. No one asked, "Who started this?" No one asked, "Who is the organizer of this activity?" Who started it was unimportant. Who the first in line was didn't matter. Each joined without question, prompted by the Spirit. This is what God is requiring of us in these last days.

Sometimes, in order to flow together, you have to concentrate on Jesus and leave the rest to Him. Speak of the glory of God. For the sake of *"the wheat, the wine and the oil,"* we must set aside our differences and flow together.

God is not nearly as issue-oriented as we are. He sees the overall picture, not just one piece of the puzzle. Let us not argue anymore about these points. Let us not be separated by insignificant matters. Let us flow together for the sake of the Kingdom of God.

When I went away from home to hold my first revival at the age of sixteen, my father told me that every church does things differently and that it was not my responsibility to change the way they did things. My only responsibility was to bless the people when it came my time to minister. I have attempted to heed that wise advice.

Lay aside whatever is hindering you from flowing together with your brothers and get out into the full rush of God's stream. Let the river flow.

Heavenly Father,

Thank You for teaching us how to flow together. We no longer want to be separate streams. We want to flow together and become the River of Your purposes in all the Earth.

In Jesus' name,
Amen!

Chapter 18

Delighting in the Glory

Then shalt thou delight thyself in the L<small>ORD</small>*; and I will cause thee to ride upon the high places of the earth, and feed thee with the heritage of Jacob thy father: for the mouth of the* L<small>ORD</small> *hath spoken it.*   Isaiah 58:14

God wants us to delight in Him, to delight in His presence, to delight in His plan, and to delight in His dealings with us on a daily basis. Learn to delight in the glory of the Lord.

We are to be a people full of delight. This is one of the most important things we can do to promote revival. If we maintain a spirit full of delight, God will promote us.

Promotion does not come from the east or the west, from the north or the south, but promotion comes from the Lord. The lifting up is of the Lord. Therefore, we must delight in God, delight in His ways, and delight in His people.

When the Queen of Sheba went up to Jerusalem to see the wisdom of Solomon, she was so impressed that she began to praise the king and everything that pertained to him. She even praised his servants, saying: *"Blessed are they that wait upon the king."* Even the servants were blessed. So we must not only delight in the Lord, but we must delight in His people as well.

We must delight in those who *"stand in His presence."* We must delight in those who *"serve Him day and night."*

The joy of the Lord that is coming forth in revival is so important that we must ask God to help us not to attempt to analyze it, but just to enjoy it. If you have never experienced the joy of the Lord, it's time to have that experience. If you have never received holy laughter, it's time for you to receive.

You may want to continue to do things in the way you have always done them, but God is saying that it's time for a new way. Get into the flow of the river so that God can cause rivers of living water to flow out of your innermost being to others.

Joy is one of the ways God strengthens us. He has chosen it as His strengthening measure. I'm not sure why, and you and I might do it differently, but that is God's choice. Joy brings strength:

> *Then he said unto them, Go your way, eat the fat, and drink the sweet, and send portions unto them for whom nothing is prepared: for this day is holy unto our Lord: neither be ye sorry; for the joy of the LORD is your strength.*
>
> Nehemiah 8:10

The joy of the Lord is your strength, and the joy of the Lord is my strength. God has placed this strengthening agent into our lives so that we will have sufficient strength for the great ingathering, the harvest that God is calling us to bring in in this last day. We must let God do it in His own way.

Some people have to be knocked to the floor the first time they laugh in the Spirit. They can't seem to do it any other way. Afterward, God can give them the spirit of laughter without having to knock them to the floor. When they feel that spirit coming upon them, they just yield to it and move on out into the flow.

If you have to be knocked out in order to do some of these things, then get knocked out often enough so that it becomes easier and easier. Eventually you won't need the help.

Last weekend, I stepped up to the pulpit to speak, and suddenly couldn't say a word. I was caught up in sort of a standing trance, seemingly frozen in place. It seemed like a trance, yet I was standing, and it must have gone on for about half an hour. I was positioned so that it was not convenient for anyone else to step up and continue the service or do anything else, for that matter. The people were respectfully waiting for me to preach, and when I came to myself, I was saying over and over again, "Blind eyes shall be opened; deaf ears shall be unstopped; and the dead shall be raised to life again."

Sometimes we have to wonder if we don't look absolutely silly in such circumstances, but we must not be unduly concerned about it. As if to prove that fact, some of the people who were in the meeting that night said that it was probably the greatest meeting they had ever been in. There was such an awesome sense of the presence of God, and we all had a new awareness of the types of miracles God was about to do in our midst in the near future.

The first time I experienced being frozen in place standing was in April of 1997. I was in Mandan, North Dakota, a town that adjoins Bismarck, and it was the first night of a series of meetings at the Bethel Assembly of God church there. As the pastor introduced me, I rose from the first row of the auditorium where I had been sitting and started to walk toward the pulpit, but before I could get there, I found myself suddenly frozen in place. Not only was I frozen in place, but I was unable to speak, so I couldn't tell anyone what was happening to me.

The pastor was waiting on the platform for me to come forward, the entire congregation was expecting to hear from me now, and there I was stuck between the front row and the altar, as the minutes rolled by. I'm not sure just how long I stayed there like that; but, perhaps because of the circumstances, it seemed like eternity. Finally, the Lord released by tongue, and I said, "I'm stuck, I can't move," and, of course, everyone broke into laughter. It was several minutes before the Lord released me to walk the rest of the way to the platform.

A man came by that night and told us that the night before he had been driving by and had seen from the highway a terrible fire in the city. He was in a hurry to get somewhere and was unable to stop to see what damage was done to the building he saw being consumed by flame, but that morning he was able to stop to see what damage had been done. To his amazement, it was the church where he had seen the fire, and it hadn't been damaged at all. The people of the church had been gathered praying for revival and God had allowed that great manifestation of fire to come forth. No wonder I had felt such glory there that I had been stuck in place! From that time on, I have been frozen in place many times, usually when I least expect it, sometimes several times in a single service, and always for at least a minute or two, and sometimes longer.

Frozen in place doesn't seem like a good description of this phenomenon because there is so much of the fire of God involved. Maybe stuck in place is a better description of what we are experiencing.

Many of us have fallen under the power of God and not been able to get up when we tried. It is happening increasingly under those circumstances, but also when we are standing or sitting because of the increased presence of God's glory in our midst and His desire to perform signs and wonders for us.

One night during our campmeeting this past summer, one of the young girls in attendance was out under the power of God and, when one of the brothers was called to help her get up from the floor, he found that he couldn't move her — as much as he tried. She was very petite, smaller than his own four daughters, but she seemed to weigh four hundred pounds or more with the weight of glory that was upon her. It was much later before he was able to get her up.

Several years ago, I was in Pretoria, South Africa. I had been invited to speak three nights at a certain church on the subject of Praise, Worship and Glory. There was a good crowd of about a thousand or more people present and we enjoyed God's presence together.

The third night, when I spoke on the Glory and invited people forward to experience it, I was expecting us to have a rather quiet standing-in-the-glory, seeing-visions-of-the-Lord and visions-of-the-heavenlies night. This seemed to be the type of altar service that was in keeping with my teaching that night. But as the people gathered around the altar, something very different began to unfold. To my right, I saw the cloud of God's glory coming into our midst. The pastor was standing several steps below me, and I called him to come quickly and see what I was seeing.

He rushed back up to the platform, and I pointed toward the glory cloud and said to him, "Look!" No sooner had I uttered that word than a group of some fifty to a hundred people fell under the power of God. As the cloud made its way toward us, in a zigzag pattern, more and more people fell under its power, in small groups. No one had prayed for them; it was a sovereign act of God as that glory cloud came in.

No sooner had people fallen in the Spirit than they would begin to burst forth in a most amazing laughter. This was new to them, and I had not spoken about it, nor had I anticipated it happening in this way. This went on for a very long time, and hours later people were still trying to find their legs and arms, and gather themselves up and get up off the floor. One very sophisticated lady told me at lunch the next day that she had been forced to crawl to a pole so that she could pull herself up. She seemed to be incapable of getting up any other way, such an amazing power of God had been flowing through her body.

That amazing night proved to be, for me in South Africa, just the first of many amazing nights. Everywhere I went God was doing something that amazed us all. One night I was singing and suddenly noticed that I had lost my accompaniment. Amanda Vanderbilt, who had accompanied me from Jerusalem, was still seated at the piano, but she had now slumped over the instrument, overwhelmed by the power of God. One hand was moving up and down over the keyboard, but she was making no contact with the keys. I had never seen her like that before, and we have laughed about it many times since.

When I was in Utenhaag, right across from Port Elizabeth, I saw an article on the front page of the South African newspaper about the wife of a pastor in Port Elizabeth and the unusual revival that was taking place at their church. I arranged to have lunch with her so that I could learn what they were experiencing. She told me that her husband and a group of the elders from the church had flown to Singapore to attend a seminar on church growth. While they were away, the One who knows more about church growth than anyone else in the world visited the church, and those who were present experienced a sovereign work of the Holy Spirit. It was so startling that she called her husband and asked what they should do. "Don't let it stop," he said. "Keep doing whatever you're doing until we get back."

The woman was very short and, because the Lord instructed her to lay hands on the heads of all the people who were attending and pray for them, she had to have a chair that she moved along with her, standing up on it in order to reach the heads of the people. This didn't prevent them from falling under the power or of receiving the deep joy that God was pouring out upon the people of South Africa.

I spoke that night in a rather conservative Pentecostal church. My hostess, a member of the Dutch Reformed congregation, accompanied me. The South

African people are very social, and my hostess was always beautifully and meticulously dressed. Her purse and shoes always matched her outfit, which she changed several times a day.

After the message and a time of waiting in the glory, I invited those who had received some vision or revelation to come forward and share it with the others. After sharing her revelation, this sister fell under the power of God right on the platform, and this was fine — until she tried to get up. Every part of her body was able to get up except her chin, which stuck to the platform. She was a very delicate and graceful person, and she now moved herself this way and that, trying to get her chin unstuck. What a funny sight she was! And we all laughed and laughed together as she struggled to free herself. We were laughing with the joy of the Lord.

That sister was so drunk with joy that we had to carry her home after the meeting, and all through the night I could hear her laughing. The next morning she looked twenty years younger, as if she had received a total face lift. I saw her last year in a conference in Jerusalem, and she told me that her experience that night had been life changing. She has never been the same. As she told it, joy and laughter broke out in our midst and many others experienced being stuck.

This experience, the supernatural move of the Spirit, happened in place after place throughout South Africa where God sent us. In one service, God gave me a word of knowledge about someone who had one leg shorter than the other. When I called it out from the platform, a man way in the back of the church instantly had his leg lengthened. It had been, it turned out, not just a little shorter, but a lot shorter, and now it was the same length as the other.

In this realm of glory, greater and greater miracles will take place. God is bringing great transformation to the hearts of people, and He is also touching their bodies and taking care of their emotional needs.

Some people have criticized the laughing revival because of the fact that some continue to laugh during the course of the sermon. That, many consider, is irreverent. But, if we stop and consider it, there was obviously something very strange going on at the house of Cornelius while Peter was preaching there. The Scriptures declare:

> *While Peter yet spake these words, the Holy Ghost fell on all them which heard the word. And they of the circumcision which believed were astonished, as many as came with Peter, because that on the Gentiles also was poured out the gift of the Holy Ghost. For they heard them speak with tongues, and magnify God.*   Acts 10:44-46

What I have observed is that when the preacher steps forward and begins to preach, he carries such an anointing, such a glory, that it provokes a reaction from the audience. They are not laughing at him or at the words he is speaking, and they probably couldn't tell you exactly why they are laughing. Their spirits are automatically responding to the glory they hear in the preacher's voice. Their laughter is a response to the glory. Why would we think, then, that their response is not honoring the Word? Have we not considered honoring the Spirit? And if the Spirit is reaching out and causing these things to happen, then who are we to question?

It was our privilege to help, from the start, the now-famous Christian celebration of the Feast of Tabernacles in Jerusalem, and we have always attended. A couple of years ago, however, I was invited to speak in one of the services on the glory realm. The night before I was to speak the Lord gave me a wonderful song on my way to the Conference Center. He showed me that the glory realm is "the realm where the angels sing," and "the realm of the heavenly King."

When I was introduced, I got up and sang the song the Lord had given me and read my scripture and, before I realized what was happening, the glory began to break forth in our midst in laughter, something which did not normally happen in that auditorium. Now, there are times when we want this to happen, and there are other times when we might prefer that God would do it in a different way, but God takes it out of the hands of the preacher and lets us know that

He is still sovereign over all. By the end of the service a number of very conservative people were stretched out on the seats on the huge platform, and they were laughing uncontrollably. Nobody laid hands on them to pray for them, but they were being touched by the glory. God is doing things differently, and we must be willing to let Him do things His way. God told me that if I would be willing for the Spirit to work as He willed, He would put me on the great platforms of the Earth.

I have seen great healings come to people emotionally in one season of laughing in the spirit. It seemed as if all the bondages of a lifetime suddenly fled away as joy and laughter came forth by the Spirit.

Delight is joy taken to the highest realm in the Spirit. It is joy manifested in the realm of the high praises that are in our mouths.

> *Delight thyself also in the* Lord*; and he shall give thee the desires of thine heart.*   Psalm 37:4

Delight is joy expressed in the glory realm.

> *As the apple tree among the trees of the wood, so is my beloved among the sons. I sat down under his shadow with great delight, and his fruit was sweet to my taste. He brought me to the banqueting house, and his banner over me was love.*
>   Song of Songs 2:3-4

Delight has the ethereal lightness of the glory cloud. I joy in God my Savior. I delight in my Beloved.

Get dressed up in the garments of praise, and get rid of any spirit of heaviness. Don't let any slight weight hold you down. Let only the weight of glory rest upon you.

Lord,

Increase my delight in You. May the delight always be present in my relationship with You. May it be unspeakable and full of glory.

Unto Your honor,
Amen! Amen! Amen!

Chapter 19

Making Room for the Glory

*Lift up your heads, O ye gates; even lift them up,
ye everlasting doors; and the King of glory shall
come in.*   Psalm 24:9

*The glory of God is bringing revival, and if we want more
revival we must make room for the glory. This is the greatest need of the hour.*

Making room for the glory speaks not only of preparing a physical place for God to work, but it also
speaks of making preparation in every area of our
lives.

One of the ways we must make room for the glory
is in our services. *Our failure to make room for the glory
in our services is the most common reason that the glory is
not seen and experienced in church after church across
America and around the world. I believe that most of the
necessary elements are in place, but we simply don't give
God a chance. We don't make room for Him to work. We
don't make room for the glory.*

Sometimes the key is as simple as singing a chorus
one or two more times. Sometimes it is as simple as

having a short silence in which we present the opportunity for the voice of the Spirit of God to be heard
prophetically. *What hinders us is rarely something complicated. We don't have major problems that need to be
overcome, but minor adjustments that need to be made.*

I am glad that God is giving me the opportunity to
help people come into the glory. I have been blessed
to be raised in a family that has always known the
glory of God, to meet many great men and women of
faith and anointing down through the years, and to
have lived and worshiped these many years in the
city of Jerusalem. But looking back I now realize that
the secret to the ministry of so many was that they
knew how to wait on God until the glory came.

Those people never just sat and waited. William
Branham, for instance, was a former Baptist minister
who received a visitation from God and began to
move in the things of the Spirit. He was not a very
large man. When he came onto the platform, he would
stand there and talk for a while, and you knew he
was just talking. He was greeting the people and saying how happy he was to have the opportunity to be
in that place. Sometimes he rehearsed the things the
Lord had done the night before, but he was still just
talking. Anyone who didn't know better might have
wondered in those moments why they had even bothered to come hear him. There was nothing dynamic
about him.

Eventually, he would say, "I am waiting for the

angel to come." The Lord had promised him that the
angel of the Lord would stand beside him every time
he ministered, and until he felt the presence of that
angel, he would just talk and wait.

Then, suddenly, you would see a dramatic change
come over that meek, mild-looking man. His shoulders went back and his eyes lit up as with flames of
fire, and just as suddenly he began calling people out
of the audience and naming their sicknesses, their
names and addresses and their doctor's names and
bringing healing and deliverance to them.

In those moments, no one needed to hear him say,
"The angel of the Lord is here." Everyone already
knew it. A man who, only a few moments before,
looked so out of place standing before that great
crowd of people, was suddenly endued with the authority of the God of the Universe, simply because he
had been faithful to wait in the service until the glory
of the Lord was manifested.

He had a wonderful gift of vision, and he described
what he was seeing, while he was seeing it. I like that.
I wish a lot more people would get that gift. In fact,
I'm asking God to enlarge me in this area.

His visions were detailed. He saw someone in an
accident, saw how it happened, what caused it and
what the results were. He saw people in the hospital
and described the doctor who shook his head and
gave them the bad news of permanent injury. But he
knew that the very person he was describing was in

the meeting that night and he would call for them to come forward. The person would eagerly come forward, and when they did, Brother Branham would ask them, "Is what I have been saying true?"

It always was.

"Then, if God can tell me all these things," he would say, "can you believe the servant of the Lord when I say that you are healed by the power of God?" And the miracle would take place before our very eyes.

How wonderful it was! That atmosphere of glory was among the greatest I have experienced in anyone's meetings anywhere in the world, but we are now moving back into days just like that.

We are all going to become much more reverential in the future, almost tiptoeing at times in the presence of God in our services. We have been like bulls in the china shop. Feel the awesome sense of God's presence and be careful before Him.

Does that mean that we won't be shouting loudly and rejoicing? Not at all. We'll be doing that, but there will be an entering in in which we will be very careful not to do anything to break the atmosphere of glory in our midst.

God wants to lift our chins. The Psalmist said:

> *But thou, O LORD, art a shield for me; my glory,*
> *and the lifter up of mine head.*   Psalm 3:3

Sometimes it only takes a little lifting to get us into

the glory realm. Maybe your head is not way down in the pit, but you just need it to be lifted one notch higher. Sometimes all that is needed is to sing a chorus one notch slower or one notch faster. When I sense this in our own services, I don't hesitate to whisper in the ear of the person leading the worship and tell them, "Just a little slower," or "Just a little faster."

Don't be too quick to dismiss this idea. Just a little notch can make all the difference and can make room for the glory.

Those who are musical purists probably feel that there is only one right way to sing a particular song. "This song must be done at this pace," they would insist. But we must learn to pace ourselves in the glory. Forget about Earth's rhythms, and get in time with the heavenly sound. Learn to synchronize yourself with the heavenly rather than the earthly.

One brother said to me after a great crusade meeting, "Ruth, I felt like I was so close to Heaven tonight, that if I had taken one more step, I would have been there." We have many services like that in our camp. Feeling close to Heaven doesn't need to be a rare occurrence. Once we have experienced it, we can experience it again and again. Get hold of these simple truths in God and you can go higher each time.

When we each received the Holy Ghost and spoke in tongues, we didn't think we could possibly go higher than we were at that moment, but we did. God always has more for us, but we must make room for it.

There are things that we all must do to make room for the glory. We must attend good meetings where God is being glorified. We must join others in praise and worship. We must speak in tongues and allow the Spirit to work in us. We must sing in the Spirit and let the glory come.

There are also things we must not do. If you fill yourself with worldly entertainment, for example, you leave no room for the glory. There is limited storage capacity in your soul, and if you have filled that limited space with other things, God cannot do for you what He would like to do. Make room for the glory.

Most of us know what it's like to have to clean out the closet. There you see a dress or a suit that was your very favorite, but that was last year and God has given you something new, so the old must go to make room for the new. If someone had even suggested that you get rid of that garment a year ago, you wouldn't have been willing to think about it. But this is another day.

In the fall of the year in Virginia we have such beautiful foliage on our trees that people travel from all over the world to see it. If those leaves don't drop off, however, no new life can come to that tree. Our trees give up one set of leaves, however glorious they might be, to get another set, a new set. Shedding the old makes room for the new.

We can exchange one glory for another glory. We may feel, as those trees during the winter months, that we are in the bare stage, that we have lost all the former glory. But we are just getting ready for a greater glory, a higher glory.

You may feel sometimes that all the beauty has fallen from your life and is scattered on the ground around you and is being carried away with the wind. But springtime is coming, and the seasons of God are not as long as the natural seasons. He knows how to do a quick work in your life. In a single hour in your spirit, old leaves can drop off and new leaves can come. We don't have to wait months for it to happen. Even in a few moment's time God can do it for you.

God constantly amazes us with what He is doing in this day. Falling leaves make room for the coming glory. Let that old order go, so that you can lay hold of the new one. Let that lesser glory go so that you can take hold of the greater.

If you feel like you are forgetting a lot of the things you have learned, don't worry about it. God is emptying your storehouse and giving you new facts. Let new glories and new giftings come to your life.

Make room for the glory in your intellect. Make room for the glory in your emotions. Make room for the glory in every area of your being. Allow God to touch you in brand new ways and to bring the necessary changes.

One of the things I love about the outbreak of joy being experienced in this revival is that God is showing us that He can bring life to our emotions. Not only can we weep by the touch of God, but we can also laugh by the touch of God. Every emotion can be controlled by the touch of God upon us.

There is a weeping that comes only with the glory.

Some years ago I met an amateur archaeologist in Melbourne, Australia. He was an Episcopalian who was against speaking in tongues, but I befriended him. He claimed to have located the Ark of the Covenant in Jerusalem, and I heard him tell this story several times. When people asked me if I thought it was true, I could only say that every time I had heard him tell the story, he had begun to weep at exactly the same point of the story. It was a type of weeping that I recognize. It was a weeping that only comes in the glory, when one has seen the glory, heard the glory, or felt the glory. I might have been skeptical of his story otherwise, but I could not deny the emotion I witnessed in him as he told the story. He was deeply touched by his experience.

God's glory touches our deepest emotions, sometimes producing deep weeping and sometimes producing deep laughter.

Don't prevent people from dancing. David danced before the Lord with all His might. If somebody wants to dance, let them do it. If someone wants to laugh outrageously, let them laugh. It may just jump from them to the choir and before long, the whole congregation will be touched by the glory of the Lord. *It is not for us to say how the glory will affect us. We must make room for God to do in us what He wants.* It's not for us to tell God His business. He knows what He is doing.

Just the time you want to be the most dignified, God will make you do something that seems totally undignified. Let Him touch you by making room for His desire. The glory will fill your soul the moment you make room for it.

When we are praying, there must come a moment when we stop putting forth our petitions and requests, and let the glory flood in. We can be so busy talking to God, so busy telling Him our needs, so busy interceding in tongues, that He doesn't have opportunity to move on us. Relax a moment and let God have His turn. You may find yourself whistling or doing something similar while God has opportunity to do His work.

I never could whistle until the glory came upon me. Now I find myself whistling at the most unusual times. Sometimes I'm whistling and I don't even know I'm whistling. Once, in a great crusade, I was whistling away, only to open my eyes and find the television camera focused right on me.

He is our glory. He is the lifter of our heads. He is lifting us up to look completely into His face.

We are those gates of glory, and we need to be lifted. We need the entrance way into our lives to be opened wide to the King of glory so that He can come in in all His majesty. Let every door be opened. Let every gate be lifted. Let every barrier be removed. Let the King of glory in. Make way for the King! Make way for the glory! When you look up, the sounds of Heaven can find their way into your soul.

When I first got a remote control, I didn't know that you had to point it in the direction of your receiver to make it work. Sometimes if you point it in the general direction, it still won't work. You have to be more precise. Get your general direction remote control more precisely pointed. God will give you focus that will enable you to make a better connection. Don't just look anywhere. Don't just look around for help. Don't just even look up. Look into the face of Jesus.

> *This is the generation of them that seek him, that*
> *seek thy face, O Jacob. Selah.*   Psalm 24:6

Lift up your heads and be ye lifted up. If you don't have your antenna aimed in just the right direction, let the Lord tilt it a little more until it is completely attuned to His voice. It's like that slowing down or speeding up a notch. He will tilt our heads a little higher, away from the natural, away from the earthly, away from the things that take our time and attention. Be lifted up.

You are the entrance. The glory must come in through your eyes, through your ears, through your feelings, and even through your nose. Some might feel that this is extreme. But God is doing it. He sends a

smell of incense into our midst. I would not have recognized it if I hadn't been in some Orthodox church
services in Jerusalem where they use high quality incense. In our meetings no one was burning incense. It
was the glory coming in through our noses. At the
Benny Hinn crusade in Miami, the fragrance of burning incense permeated the arena and lingered there.
Thousands were blessed by this manifestation of
God's glory. Every one of our senses must make room
for the glory.

I met a very lovely lady who lives in an exclusive
suburb of Minneapolis. She has a lovely shop known
as Ribbons and Roses in the town of Wyzata. There
she sells fine stationeries, lovely gift items, and the
best perfumes. These are not found in the department
stores. She has brought them from all over the world.
She was one of the first to have freeze-dried flowers.
They're very beautiful.

We became friends and she attended our services
when I was in her area. After she had heard me and
read my book, God put it in her heart to develop a
perfume called *Glory*. In order to do this she refused
for a whole year to wear any perfume or to have any
fragrance in her house. She was believing for God to
give her and her husband the very scent of Jesus.

For about a year they refused to light scented
candles at supper time, refused to use scented soap
in the bathroom. Until one night, Jesus walked into
their house, and they could smell His fragrance. This

happened again and again until they were sure of the scent they wanted to produce.

Once they had the idea, they set off for France to speak with the perfumers there and to describe the scent they had smelled. Since the perfumers hadn't smelled the scent it has been a slow process, but they are determined to produce it and they are still working on it right now.

Maybe you can't afford to hire perfumers to make a scent for you, but you can do whatever it takes to make room for the glory in your life as well. God will give you great revelations if you give Him your full attention.

Some students think they can study and do something else at the same time. Some can listen to the radio and still study. Some can watch television and still study. But God will have a people who so desire the glory to be revealed in a greater way that they will make room for Him alone. We must make room in our schedules, make room in our time, make room for Him in every way. Sometimes we just need to pause and let those new sounds of glory come into our spirits.

The young son of a friend is pastoring a great church in the San Francisco area. He started the church two years ago and already has fifteen hundred in attendance. When we met in a great crusade, I saw a vision of him and told him what I saw. I saw him making room for the Holy Spirit to work among the people.

He had been hesitant to use the word of knowledge ministry, but I had seen the Lord changing the order of his service. I saw him stepping up and speaking by the word of knowledge and ministering to his people.

When I said that, he responded, "That's what I have been praying for."

Sometimes we pray for things and they don't happen because we're not willing to make room for them in our services. Make room for whatever the Holy Spirit wants to do.

Take your schedule, rip it up and throw it to the wind. Make time for the glory. Make room for the glory. Now we are singing:

We're making room for the glory.
We're making room for the glory.
We're making room for the glory.
The glory of the Lord.

Lord,

How I desire your glory. Show me personally what I need to do to make room for Your glory. Then help me to do it.

In Jesus' name,
Amen!

Chapter 20

Waiting in the Glory for Revelation

For our light affliction, which is but for a mo-
ment, worketh for us a far more exceeding and
eternal weight of glory; While we look not at the
things which are seen, but at the things which
are not seen: for the things which are seen are
temporal: but the things which are not seen are
eternal.   2 Corinthians 4:17-18

I encourage people to see the eternal, but each one must purpose to see, must have a desire to see and be hungry to see. And each one must believe to see and start reaching out to see. You can't see without making the effort to look.

In our campmeetings, I always enjoy hearing visiting ministers, but I enjoy, even more, the services when we have a flow of revelation in that same time frame, and I know that God wants to do it more for us. He can only give us a flow of revelation through people who have moved into the revelatory realm and desire to be used of God in this way.

I believe some of our best meetings have been when those who have just begun to move into the revelatory realm began to describe what they were seeing. It isn't always easy to describe eternal things with our limited vocabularies, but God will help us to do it. We must speak out what He is showing us, proclaiming and declaring it. It is the "now vision." It's not even the vision I had before I came to church. It's the vision I begin to reach into and take a hold of and get understanding of while I am in the realm of the Spirit. And by His help I will describe what the Lord is saying through the vision.

He is causing us to see Him, and we simply must reach out for this revelation. If He doesn't fill our vision more and more, we won't be able to make it in the days to come. He must become all-consuming in our visions.

God delights in removing the veil from our eyes and causing every scale to come off, so that we can see and see clearly His glory, the glory of His countenance. Then we will know the glory of His purposes, we will know the glory of His plan, and we will walk in realms of glory.

You don't have to have a full-fledged vision before you can share it. I have found that you receive great visions by sharing the little ones, all those little glimpses into eternity. We are like the blind man who was prayed for twice. The first time he saw men as trees walking, but he described what he saw. He didn't see the picture clearly, but if you will declare the vision, even if you don't see it in its fullness, the next time you will see more. The declaration of it re-leases something in your own spirit.

God wants us to live in the realm of vision, and we must do it in the days ahead, for it is the revelation of God that will quicken our spirits.

There are still many people who don't believe in vision, but that doesn't negate what God is doing. Despite the doubts of many, God is bringing forth the ministry of the seers, those who prophesy by vision.

The entire future of our ministries is dependent upon our ability to see into the heavenly realm, there-fore God wants to elevate us into a seeing dimension. He wants to cover us with eyes. The anointing to see will cause you to stand in high places. Let there come to you right now a keenness, a sensitivity in the realm of the Spirit. May the anointing for seeing be released in you from this day forward.

Seeing into the needs of the people will change the way you preach. We must move from the informa-tional type of preaching that comes from our accumulated wisdom and knowledge into a revela-tory preaching that comes to us at the moment. We must be as the prophet of old who opened for the first time a scroll that he had never read and began to de-clare its contents. Each of us must reach up, take the scroll and unroll it before the people. It will be fresh bread for all those who hear it.

Forget what the former strong points of your min-istry have been and start declaring the new things God gives you. Lay aside those former strong points and let your ministry be known for the strength of revelation that will come forth from it in the days ahead.

Some of you will begin to have a flow of visions and revelations as you are doing your daily tasks. You don't have to wait until you are in church to receive revelation. Believe God for it on a daily basis — wherever you happen to be and whatever you happen to be doing at the moment.

What God is showing us sometimes seems to be so simple that we wonder if we dare share it with anyone else. Simple things are often profound. Don't be afraid to share what God is telling you. It will bless someone.

God wants to reveal things to you as you walk. God wants to reveal to you the hearts of men.

Some people get frightened as they feel an unusual fluttering in their hearts. That's nothing to be worried about. The Holy Spirit is causing an eternal flutter, a quickening of the Spirit. He is teaching you.

God is leaning down to whisper secrets in your ear, first one and then the other. Take hold of what He is saying to you. Take hold of that to which He has called you. Take hold of the ministry to which He has ordained you. Take hold of the city in which He sees fit to establish you. Take hold in the realm of the Spirit.

These are days of seeing and possessing what we see.

Because God is anointing us more and more to look

into the unseen realm, look for the eternal in every service. Look for the glory. Look for the manifestation of it. Let God anoint you unto the excellence of this new day.

Just as God fed Elijah by the Brook Cherith day by day, in these last days God will take His prophets into the eternal realm and let them sit in it — day by day.

God is teaching us to handle the eternal things. He is giving us many-faceted eyes.

If we were not aware of the fact that we could experience the glory of God in every service, we could grope as men in darkness, wondering when it might come. Because we know it is available, it becomes our responsibility in every service to move into the realms of revelation so that we can bless others with the glory of God. God wants us to go from revealed glory to revealed glory.

And when he was demanded of the Pharisees, when the kingdom of God should come, he answered them and said, The kingdom of God cometh not with observation: Neither shall they say, Lo here! or, lo there! for, behold, the kingdom of God is within you. And he said unto the disciples, The days will come, when ye shall desire to see one of the days of the Son of man, and ye shall not see it. And they shall say to you, See here; or, see there: go not after them, nor follow them. For as the lightning, that lighteneth out of

*the one part under heaven, shineth unto the other
part under heaven: so shall also the Son of man
be in his day.*   Luke 17:20-24

At Winter Campmeeting this year, when some
friends traveled a long way to hear me minister, I decided to speak in the morning sessions for their
benefit, although I was not scheduled to speak. What
happened that week was glorious. God spoke to me
the words *Glory Revealed* and that became our theme
and the thing which God did in our midst. This is the
hour of the glory of God revealed, and the only way
that glory is manifested is by revelation. It comes no
other way.

What was Jesus saying in this passage? He was saying that there was a revelatory realm that comes forth
"like the lightnings under the heaven." Lightning happens with great frequency, and is a most natural
occurrence. Sometimes we perceive it and sometimes
we don't. If we are looking in the right direction when
the lightning pierces the sky, we may see it. At other
times, we don't see it, but we hear the noise it produces, so we know it is present. Many times, however,
we neither see it or hear it. It happens so quickly that
we miss it, as powerful as it is.

When Jesus was on the Earth, He was easily visible. If He was present, men knew it. Now, however,
His presence is much like that lightning. It shines out
of one part of Heaven unto another part of Heaven,

and many are unaware that it has even been manifested.

Lightning is spoken of in other important passages.
Revelation 4 and Ezekiel 1 both speak of the lightnings that come forth from the throne of God. I believe
this speaks to us of the quickenings of revelation that
God is giving us in these days.

We are so blessed in this generation to have video
machines that allow us to play and replay a certain
tape that we like or want to learn from. With just a
press of the button we can see it all again. If we miss
some detail, we can just hit the rewind switch and
look at the part we are interested in again if we want.
In fact, if we want to see it a hundred times, we can
see it a hundred times. How blessed we are!

God is looking for people who can receive the lightning experiences of revelation. They come so quickly
and are gone, but those who are keen in the Spirit will
receive that touch of eternity and cling to it.

We must have the eyes of our spirit sensitized more
and more so that we can lay hold of the revelations of
God as they come forth. This great revival is bringing
forth great revelation. It is coming as we sit in the
cloud of God's glory.

I love revelatory services, in which, one after another, we all prophesy by revelation and by vision.
When it's not happening, I get a few of our most spiritual leaders together and encourage them to believe
for it, to flow in it.

If you want great revelation, you have to believe for it. Then, make yourself available and watch what God will do.

Revelation will bring you the understanding of where to go from here, what step to take next, and how to handle the current situation.

You will notice in the meetings of Benny Hinn and others that they are beginning to talk more and more of the need for revelation. He has wonderful revelations himself and he believes it is for everyone.

As the glory is revealed in our midst, Jesus is revealed. Isaiah said, "I see the Lord," and you can say it too. This is not a onetime experience. God wants to reveal Himself to you every day, in progressions. The nature of revelation is *"precept upon precept, line upon line, here a little and there a little."* It's very much like placing the blocks in a building. Piece by piece, it takes form, until, one day, we will have the completed revelation.

> *For now we see through a glass, darkly; but then face to face: now I know in part; but then shall I know even as also I am known.*
>
> 1 Corinthians 13:12

I met a brother in South Africa who had some wonderful heavenly experiences. He was caught away in the heavens again and again. We spoke for several hours and I understood what he was saying although

I had never been caught away for such long periods of time. I realized later that it was because of the many lightning experiences I have had with God that what the brother was saying did not seem foreign to me at all.

Perhaps, one day soon, we will see it all together at one time. Some people are seeing much more than others. They just seem to be blessed with an ability to yield to God for revelation.

We shouldn't get up too quickly from the altar or from falling under the power of God. If you have no reason to get up quickly, linger for a while. Give God the opportunity to reveal Himself to you. If you have tried it and nothing seemingly happened, keep on trying until it does. This is one revelation you simply can't miss.

What we see in the Spirit is often like peripheral vision. We can see clearly what is directly ahead of us. Many things, however, pass by on to the side and we don't perceive them very clearly. I see visions while I am preaching and while I am praying for people. I might be looking at the people and focusing on them, but God is giving me something else to see in my peripheral vision. I learned to give attention to it and to focus on it, while focusing on the people. Become sensitive to His desires.

Isaiah said, *"The glory of God shall be revealed and all flesh shall see it together."*

When someone in charge of a service begins to flow

in vision, reach out in the Spirit so that you can flow with them. Just as we worship as one voice, and we reach out together for prophetic messages, and could sometimes tell the next words or phrases of a prophetic message even before they are spoken by another person, likewise we can flow together in vision. We can see the same thing at the same time.

We began to experience this in Jerusalem and twenty or more people were seeing the same thing at the same moment. When we began to share our experiences, not everyone described them the same. And that's quite normal.

When a group of people are watching television together, one is focusing on what a particular person is doing on the screen, while still another may be focusing on what is being said rather than what is being done. We are all seeing the same thing, but we are describing it in different ways.

When we would share our vision, one person would say, "I saw a river flowing, but suddenly it seemed to stop."

Another person would say, "In my vision, it didn't stop. It went on until I saw it cascade over a waterfall."

For many years, every night we experienced a great variety of revelations, and many times we discovered that we were all seeing the same thing at the same time.

When you see the fire of God, don't immediately

think of the fires of persecution. Let God's flames begin to consume you with Himself, with His presence and with His glory. Fire is one of the manifestations of the glory of God and we're going to see it more and more, so get used to it and stop associating it with things that should be burned up and destroyed.

As He has done in the past, God is giving His people dreams and visions through this revival. These dreams and visions are not just nice possibilities. We should expect the fulfillment of every single one of them.

Another thing that we should expect more of in this revival is to see the angels of God. I was in a meeting in Winterville, North Carolina, one night not so long ago, and I saw something I had never seen before. Angels were doing a Jericho March around the outside of the church. They were lined up in precise formation, as if in perfect ranks and, one behind the other, marched around the building.

The next morning, I saw two angels standing outside the door of the church. They turned one way and then another calling the people to come to the service. When I told the pastors, Art and Barbara Delano, what I had seen, they told me that they and their people had been believing for it, and that, indeed, their attendance has been increasing.

Every great revival has experienced such angelic activity, and we should expect to see it more in the coming days.

Many times people tell me, "Sister Ruth, when I first got saved and filled with the Spirit, I had wonderful visions. But I was told that they were not from God, so I stopped yielding to God in that way and asked Him to take that gift from me. Now I know that what I was experiencing was God and that He was showing me wonderful things and I regret not having continued in them."

For many years these people were robbed of vision because they were afraid to let the Spirit of God flow freely in their lives.

Vision is just one aspect of revelation. There are other new things God is doing in our lives which often cause fear in many. If we don't have a frame of reference by which to judge something, we are afraid of it.

The one phrase I taught our people in Jerusalem over and over again was: "You can trust the Holy Spirit." Nothing could be more important.

The angel Gabriel appeared to Mary and to Joseph without their seeking for it. The wise men, however, were already looking at the star. They were already looking, and in the midst of their looking, revelation came to them, that one of those stars was moving. And not only was it moving, but they needed to follow it.

You can experience both types of revelation. One is sovereign and the other comes through seeking and searching for God. If you really want the great things of God in your soul, you must be one who longs to know the Lord in a greater way.

Notice how many times in scripture the prophets asked angels, "What is this? (What does this mean?)" Zachariah was one those who had this dialogue with an angel. He was not just hearing what the angel was saying. He was asking specific questions.

When John saw the revelation of Jesus there were aspects he didn't understand, so he asked for clarification. He not only saw things, he was given the interpretation of what he was seeing. He not only saw the candlesticks and the stars in the hand of the Lord, but then it was explained to him that the candlesticks were the seven churches and that the stars he had seen were the messengers to the churches.

> *The mystery of the seven stars which thou sawest in my right hand, and the seven golden candle-sticks. The seven stars are the angels of the seven churches: and the seven candlesticks which thou sawest are the seven churches.*
>
> Revelation 1:20

We must ask. We must look. We must knock. We must ponder. We must let God reveal the answer to us.

A lady from New York came to our campmeeting because of a dream. "What did you dream, Sister?" I asked her.

She said, "I dreamed of a place that had many different doors, and I came because God spoke to me that this place would open many doors for me."

After she got to the camp, she had a vision of many different keys. When she inquired of the Lord what the keys meant, He told her, "It's not enough just to have the doors. You need the keys to open those doors."

God's showing us, by His Spirit, the ease in which He's bringing forth revival in this last day and hour. We can have entire weeks of glory, when many move into new realms of the Spirit of God and let His river flow. I'm not disturbed when we don't have preaching in a service. I'd be very happy for one person to start prophesying and flow into the next. I was so happy when the teacher of the adult women's Sunday school class in our campmeeting sang her entire Sunday school lesson in the Spirit one day. It was wonderful!

God is doing things differently, and if we are willing to move with His flow, we don't have to return to old patterns. We can move into new patterns by the revelation of the Spirit of the Living God.

God might interrupt some of your plans, and He just might turn your plans upside down.

We can know by the Spirit of the Lord.

Can we trust the Holy Spirit? Absolutely, we can trust Him.

Those who ignore visions are only robbing themselves. And if you have ever given a gift that was not appreciated, you probably didn't try as hard to please that person the next time around.

If you want the revelation of the Spirit flowing in your life, appreciate what God's saying to you, even when you don't understand it all. God is not just giving us little things to titillate us, to tickle our ears or to make us feel happy. He is showing us great things, eternal things, in the Spirit, things that have the potential to change the course of history in many nations for His glory.

Did John receive the entire revelation in one sitting or were there many unfoldings? My own experience has been the limited, unfolding of revelation, so I am of the opinion that John received his revelation in that way. Others, however, believe that John received his revelation in one long vision. I'm not sure that it matters. Either way, God wants us to be a people of the revelation of the Holy Spirit.

Vision is one of the most important methods God is using to reveal Himself to the Church today. Many people have a problem with vision because it generally happens so quickly and passes. We would prefer that it be like a movie that lasts much longer, that it contain much more detail, and that we be given much more time to ponder it. But, whether it happens that way or not, don't ever take vision for granted. Don't ever take the audible voice of God in your spirit for granted. Don't ever become blasé about the dreams He gives you in the night season.

Some people can say, "I can have a vision any time I want." Well, those people are blessed, and they should consider the preciousness of their gift. It is to be treasured. Some people have the ability to make large sums of money. They should appreciate that fact because other people have to make a great effort just to pay their bills on time.

When God gives you some greater ability, don't ever take it for granted. Appreciate it. Too many people who have received great abilities in the realm of the Spirit have done less with those abilities than those who have received little. Sometimes when we have only a little ability we appreciate it more and use it more.

I don't see as many visions as some, but I talk about every one I get. I get excited about them and reach out to understand what God is showing me and apply it.

While it is true that we spent many exciting years overseas, it is also true that our greatest adventures for God began in the most simple way, with a simple revelation. Once we had learned that secret, we continued to live by revelation.

We can pray, "God, reveal what we need to know about this subject by your Spirit. Reveal what we need to know about this situation by Your Spirit."

When we were children, we moved often, and, unlike those who move on a whim, my parents were always praying to know where the Lord wanted us to move. We moved only by revelations.

We never once moved based on what we could afford. We never once moved based on seeing a house the family liked and wanted to live in. Unless God showed us when and where, we didn't move. No wonder we have been so blessed!

God didn't give all the revelations to me directly, but I became good at listening to the revelations everyone else was having and many times they were for my instruction as well. Be humble enough to receive from others. Some will only receive from certain individuals, but they limit themselves in this way. Recognize the voice of God, even if he uses a rooster or a donkey to speak to you. Whenever God has quickened something to my spirit, I have been off and running with it.

There are certain things that God sovereignly shows you, without your having to ponder them. After I had that revelation of the moments dropping down, I lived in that revelation all that day. It was such an amazing, sovereign thing that God had done, without my having pondered them at all.

There are other times when we begin a spiritual search concerning something of God, something you're interested in, something you're moving toward, something you want God to reveal to you.

We ladies can get tenacious when we are searching

for something we want to buy. If we don't find it in one store, we look in another one. If it's not in the first ten stores we look in, we ask someone about it, and when they tell us it can be found across town, we can't wait for an opportunity to go there.

"No," they tell us, "We used to have it, but we don't carry it anymore. You might find it at ..." And we go off searching in another direction.

Men are like that with tools. They buy more tools to do more things that never get done.

We know how to search things out in the natural and we don't give up. If we really want something, we don't give up searching for it. We have that thing in our minds to give somebody for Christmas, and we're not going to give them anything else but that. If we have to go a hundred miles out of the way to that little shop that we saw it in when we were passing that way once, we go all the way back there and get that little gift.

God wants us to have that same tenacity of spirit in seeking Him. He wants us to search out these wonderful things until we are satisfied.

It's wonderful when you're in the Spirit and what you know is not by the understanding of the flesh. It's exciting to be on the cutting edge of what God is doing, to know that you're not trained in that way in the natural, but that God has just put you in the middle of it in the Spirit. God will put us in the middle of things for which we have no natural background.

We want to know the Lord according to revelation rather than according to our human understanding. We want to know the Holy of Holies, not architecturally speaking, but according to experience.

Living in Israel has been quite an experience because of all the learned Jewish men who are there, more than anywhere else in the world. These men know all the original languages of the Bible and can tell you what every commentator and rabbi has said on every word of it. Jesus mentioned the *"jots"* and the *"tittles,"* and these men can tell you exactly where they belong. How could you feel comfortable around such learned men? Because when you have worshiped, you know what you know by the Spirit. When you have searched out the deeper things of God, you have nothing to fear.

And to think that you didn't even know what to search out. Most of us don't even know the question, let alone the answer. God knows how to show us what the *"eye hath not seen,"* what the *"ear hath not heard,"* and what the heart *"[hath] not perceived."*

How can unsaved people read the Bible without being saved? Because it comes by revelation. How can born again people read the Bible without being filled with the Spirit? Because it comes by revelation. How can sick people read the Bible without being healed? Because it comes by revelation.

If God gives you a jewel that no one else appreciates please don't throw it away. Many Americans have little appreciation for the unfamiliar gems of South Africa. How many Americans have ever seen a yellow diamond? How many Americans have ever seen a green diamond? Unless you go to the Smithsonian Institute, you may never see these things. That doesn't nullify the fact that they are more rare and, therefore, more costly than the more common blue diamonds. The fact that most people, if given the choice, would pick the type of diamond they are most accustomed to seeing, doesn't negate the worth of the other.

Determine in your heart to search out the deeper things of God. He desires to have a people that sits and ponders. Most of the time, when I'm riding in the car, I'm pondering, like Mary:

> *Mary kept all these things, and pondered them*
> *in her heart.*   Luke 2:19

I'm a news person, because of my care and concern for the nations and because of my prophetic anointing, and I enjoy watching the plans and purposes of God being revealed in the news. If I'm traveling up to Washington, I listen to the twenty-four-hour-a-day news station. I'm a CNN junkie. I also like C-Span because it gives me a glimpse of what is happening on Capitol Hill. Other than the news and a few Christian programs, I prefer to take any time available to me to ponder the deeper things of God, to consider the things of the Spirit.

Daddy said that people try to do by understanding what the Holy Spirit wants to do by revelation, that people want to do with definitions of words and the study of many translations what is actually the work of the Spirit, which is to reveal the Word of God to you as you read, study and stand in the glory. In earlier days of revival, people were much more dependent on the Holy Spirit for revelation. One humble pastor had an angel that came to him daily and taught him the Scriptures. He was illiterate, but God saw the hunger in his heart, and he became a great preacher.

Lord,

You are opening our eyes to see You, to see Your glory, to see the heavenlies, to see Your glory manifested here and among the nations. We thank you for it.

In Jesus' name,
Amen!

The Ultimate Revival

Chapter 21

Seeing Jesus in the Glory

But the people that do know their God shall be strong, and do exploits.　　　　Daniel 11:32

And their eyes were opened, and they knew him.
　　　　　　　　　　　　　　　　Luke 24:31

We are seeing great miracles performed in the glory, but this revival is not just for the miraculous. *The ultimate revival is the revelation of Jesus Christ.* The first phrase of the book of Revelation sums up the whole book, *"the revelation of Jesus Christ."*

You might say, "I already know Him." You may know Him in measure, but there are many other realms of knowing to which we will soon be introduced. You may know Him, but you will know Him and know Him and know Him some more — until, at last you KNOW Him. Knowing Him is the ultimate revival, knowing Him in the glory.

We begin by knowing Him as Savior. We come to know Him as the Baptizer in the Holy Ghost. Then we come to know Him as Great Physician, the Healer. We begin to know Him as Jehovah Jireh, the Great

Provider. All this is just the beginning of knowing, of knowing who He really is. There is much yet to be revealed, and as we follow on to know Him, we will discover Him in one new dimension after another. The glory reveals Him. It brings forth *"the revelation of Jesus Christ."*

John was already an old man when he was banished to the Isle of Patmos. In his youth, he had leaned his head upon the bosom of Jesus. What a privilege! As a very young man he had experienced revival. He not only witnessed the Lord in the flesh, he also witnessed the outpouring of the Holy Ghost at Pentecost, the outpouring of the Spirit that came at Caesarea ten years later, and the outpouring of the Spirit that came at Ephesus twenty years later. All through his life, he had seen God working miraculously. Still, in his twilight years, we find him reaching out for more, this time for *"the revelation of Jesus Christ."*

If any man knew the Lord, it was John. He knew what Jesus had done on the Earth and what His disciples had done in His name. He knew Him in the flesh and, perhaps more than any of the other disciples, he knew Him in the Spirit. Still he sensed that there was a greater revelation awaiting him. As Solomon had more songs, one thousand and one altogether, but was given the song of all songs, so John is given the revelation of all revelations, *"the revelation of Jesus Christ."*

In our Winter Campmeeting early this year, one

morning I had an experience very much like Ezekiel, and I turned quickly to his prophecy:

> *And above the firmament that was over their heads was the likeness of a throne, as the appearance of a sapphire stone: and upon the likeness of the throne was the likeness as the appearance of a man above upon it. And I saw as the colour of amber, as the appearance of fire round about within it, from the appearance of his loins even upward, and from the appearance of his loins even downward, I saw as it were the appearance of fire, and it had brightness round about. As the appearance of the bow that is in the cloud in the day of rain, so was the appearance of the brightness round about. This was the appearance of the likeness of the glory of the Lord. And when I saw it, I fell upon my face, and I heard a voice of one that spake.* Ezekiel 1:26-28

Like Ezekiel, I saw the Heavens opened, and I saw the Lord *"from the appearance of His loins even downward."* That's not always the way He reveals Himself. We come to know Him by seeing Him reveal Himself in various ways. This doesn't mean that we are seeing Him in a limited way. Nothing about God is limited. We can know Him by seeing His hands. We can know Him by seeing His feet. He shows us what we need to see at the moment.

That particular day I saw the Lord from the waist down, and He was seated on His throne. Something about the way He sat there spoke to me. I didn't need to see His hand extending a scepter to know that He was King. There was majesty in the way He sat upon the throne. No wonder John declares through the corridors of time: *"unto Him that sitteth upon the throne"* (Revelation 5:13).

If you have seen the statue of Abraham Lincoln in the Lincoln Memorial in Washington, D.C., you know that there is a greatness about the way Lincoln sits there. Even if you don't read his powerful words inscribed on the walls behind him, you have seen enough to know that he was a great and powerful man. From the sitting alone you sense the greatness and the authority that was his.

That's the way I saw the Lord. I didn't see His clothing on that occasion. I saw nothing of the ornamentation and grandeur of His kingly robes. I just saw the glory of His sitting, yet in that moment, I realized that although kingdoms may come and kingdoms may go, there is an eternal glory to our God seated on His throne. How could we ever have a worry or a fear or a concern in the face of His seated majesty?

After my brother died, some wondered if the ministry of the church and the campground would continue, but I didn't stay awake even one night worrying about it. I have seen the Lord, so how can I ever worry again? I didn't get immediately into the accounts payable to see what the needs of the ministry might be. I had seen the Lord; what did I have to fear? When you have seen the glory of the Lord upon the throne, nothing can ever cause you to fear again. I had seen the King upon His throne; why should I be concerned for the future? If you haven't moved into that revelation yet, do it today. It doesn't take long.

Once you have seen the Lord you will be compelled to allow His fire to burn in you, and one of the reasons you do that is because you want to continue to see Him. You want the seeing of Him to be a continual experience.

Although, on this occasion, I only saw Him from the waist down, I instantly knew that He was totally in control, that He rules over the affairs of this world, and I knew that He was bringing forth revival.

Revival is bringing an acceleration of the purposes of God in the Earth, and an important part of that revival is the revealing to us of our Bridegroom. The revelation of Jesus Christ is a very personal thing. It's not enough for you to read what I have seen or what others have seen. You can hear someone else speak of their experiences in Heaven, but it's not enough. Unless you are seeing in the realm of the Spirit yourself, you won't be satisfied. You will only be frustrated. But you don't have to be. God is doing it so easily for all of us.

You don't have to be someone special to receive this revelation. In some of the smaller congregations where people are relatively unknown, they are experiencing wonderful revelation. With some of those who are not having a revelation of the Lord, it is because they are not taking time to seek Him. They feel that they just don't have time to wait in the presence of the Lord. "We don't even have enough time to read the Word," they say, "let alone wait for the interpretation of it." But nothing could be more important than the revelation of Jesus. When you have seen Him, great truths can be made known to you, even without reading.

In the anointing, say to the Lord, "Would You show me something wonderful about Yourself that I've never known before? Would you reveal some little aspect of Your character to me? Could I see Your hands close up?"

Does the Lord have time to be with you? Absolutely. We know that He is great and that *the heaven of heavens cannot contain him.* But we also know that He delighted to sit down by the woman at the well and commune with her heart to heart. And He will do the same for you.

Begin to notice how many times in His earthly ministry Jesus took time to deal with individuals. There were crowds, but He was interested in the individuals within those crowds. There were multitudes, but He loved the individuals within those multitudes. He revealed great truths to the crowds, but He was just as concerned to reveal great truths to the individuals in those crowds.

He did not deal only with the scholarly or the great.

He loved the little people, the new people, the common people. The greatest revelation of the ministry of Jesus — other than that given to Nicodemus — came to this woman at the well, a woman who was not even Jewish, a woman who had gone through five husbands and the man she was living with at the moment was not one of the five. It was to this woman that Jesus gave the revelation of true worship. If you are willing to ponder the deep things of God, He is willing to stop by your well and reveal Himself to you. Say to Him, "I want to consider You, Lord."

It takes a Hubble Telescope for man to see the farthest stars, but you and I, in a moment's time, can be carried to the very throne of God. Scientists needed that telescope to reach out to the farthest parts of our universe, but in a moment you and I can be carried away in the Spirit and, suddenly, we are there, and we are seeing like John saw:

> *After this I looked, and, behold, a door was opened in heaven: and the first voice which I heard was as it were of a trumpet talking with me; which said, Come up hither, and I will show thee things which must be hereafter. And immediately I was in the spirit; and, behold, a throne was set in heaven, and one sat on the throne.*

Revelation 4:1-2

Jim Irwin and other astronauts had the privilege of

standing on the moon, but you and I can stand on *"the sea of glass."* We can dance on that sea before the throne in anointed meetings.

Some people say to me, "Sister Ruth, I'm just glad to know enough to get a couple of people saved," but you don't want to go to Heaven with just a little knowledge of Him. You want to know Him, and you want to be ready for the Marriage of the Lamb.

In some countries marriages are arranged, and couples are united without first having the opportunity of knowing much about each other. Most of us don't like that idea at all. We want to know the intimate details about a person beforehand. We want to know the secrets of their hearts before we are willing to commit ourselves to them for life.

The Lord, our heavenly Bridegroom, is willing to reveal His secrets to us through the Spirit. This is the day of revelation. This is the day of God's glory. This is the day when God wants to make Himself known to us.

When you love someone, you want to know everything you can about that person. It isn't enough just to look at them. Your heart yearns to know more and more. Later, when first love begins to wane, a couple may lose interest in each other's opinions on various subjects. They've heard enough. That's why the Lord tells us to live in *"first love,"* where everything, even the simplest revelation, is a jewel.

The wife wants to know what the husband did as a

boy, and he wants to know her experiences as a girl. They want to know everything about each other. In first love, they never tire of hearing the same experiences recounted again and again. With each retelling the love grows stronger.

These are days of love for the Body of Christ. We are not only learning to know the King in His majesty, but we are also coming to know Him as Bridegroom and Lover, the Beloved of our souls. There are many things that we want to consider about Him, and all these we learn to know in Revival Glory.

Lord,

My eyes have seen, my ears have heard, my heart has perceived; for You have revealed Yourself to me in revival glory. My desire is to know You more. Continue to reveal Yourself to me.

In Jesus' name I pray,
Amen!

Books by Ruth Ward Heflin

Revival Glory   ISBN 1-8842369-80-4 $13.00

Glory   English Edition   ISBN 1-884369-00-6 ... 10.00
      Spanish Edition   ISBN 1-884369-15-4 ... 10.00
      French Edition   ISBN 1-884369-41-3 ... 10.00
      German Edition   ISBN 1-884369-16-2 ... 10.00
      Swedish Edition   ISBN 1-884369-38-3 ... 10.00
      Finnish Edition   ISBN 1-884369-75-8 ... 10.00
      Korean Edition   ISBN 1-884369-52-9 ... 10.00

Jerusalem, Zion, Israel and the Nations
                    ISBN 1-884369-05-7 ... 12.00

I Ask for the Nations   ISBN 1-884369-81-2 ... 10.00

Order at:

Calvary Books
11352 Heflin Lane
Ashland, VA 23005
(804) 798-7756

www.revivalglory.org

Or ask for them at your favorite bookstore.

God of Miracles

Eighty Years of the Miraculous

by Edith Ward Heflin

"My life has been very exciting because I was always looking forward to the next miracle, the next answer to prayer, the next thing Jesus would do for me. I expect I have lived twenty lifetimes within these eighty years. The God of all miracles has been so good and so very gracious to me."

– Edith Heflin

As you become witness to a life that has spanned the period from Azuza Street to this next great revival, the life of a unique woman who has known the great ministries of our century and has herself lived the life of the miraculous, you too will encounter the God of Miracles.

ISBN 1-56043-043-5 .... $10.00

Calvary Books
11352 Heflin Lane
Ashland, VA 23005
(804) 798-7756
www.revivalglory.org

Or ask for them at your favorite bookstore.

Hear the Voice of God

by
Wallace H. Heflin, Jr.

* Does God still speak to His people as He did to the prophets of old?
* If so, how does He speak?
* Can we actually hear His voice?
* What can we do to become more sensitive to God's voice?

Wallace Heflin Jr. spent a lifetime hearing the voice of God and following God's directives in dynamic ministry to the people of this nation and the world. In this manuscript, the last one that he prepared before his death in December of 1996, he challenges us that not only is it possible to hear the voice of God, but that God actually extends to every one of us an invitation to commune with Him.

ISBN 1-884369-36-7 .... $13.00

Calvary Books
11352 Heflin Lane
Ashland, VA 23005
(804) 798-7756
www.revivalglory.org

Or ask for them at your favorite bookstore.

The Power of Prophecy

by
Wallace H. Heflin, Jr.

"Of all the nine gifts of the Spirit, prophecy is the gift that God is using most to bring in the revival of the end-time. Because of that, it is prophecy that is being opposed now more than any other gift. I want to declare that it is time to take the limits off the gift of prophecy and off the prophets God has raised up for this hour. It is time to move into God's plan of action to declare His will prophetically to this, the final generation."

– Rev. Wallace Heflin, Jr.

- What is prophecy?
- What does it accomplish?
- Who can prophesy?
- How can YOU get started prophesying?

These and many other important questions are answered in this unique and timely volume.

ISBN 1-884369-22-7 .... $10.00

Calvary Books
11352 Heflin Lane
Ashland, VA 23005
(804) 798-7756
www.revivalglory.org

Or ask for them at your favorite bookstore.

Other books
by
Rev. Wallace H. Heflin, Jr.

A Pocket Full of Miracles	0-914903-23-3	7.00
Bride, The	1-884369-10-3	7.00
Jacob and Esau	1-884369-01-4	7.00
Potter's House, The	0-914903-91-8	7.00
Power In Your Hand	0-914903-64-0	7.00
Power In Your Hand (*Spanish Edition*)	1-884369-04-9	6.00

Calvary Books
11352 Heflin Lane
Ashland, VA 23005
(804) 798-7756
www.revivalglory.org

Or ask for them at your favorite bookstore.

Jerusalem, Israel, Zion and the Nations

by
Ruth Ward Heflin

"God is returning the focus once again to Jerusalem. The place of beginnings is also the place of endings. And God's endings are always glorious.

"This overview is by no means definitive but an unfolding of scriptures coming into prominence in these days. As Moses saw the Promised Land from Nebo, one sees the world from Jerusalem."

— Ruth Heflin

ISBN 1-884369-05-7 .... $12.00

Calvary Books
11352 Heflin Lane
Ashland, VA 23005
(804) 798-7756
www.revivalglory.org

Or ask for them at your favorite bookstore.

Calvary Pentecostal Tabernacle

11352 Heflin Lane
Ashland, VA 23005

Tel. (804) 798-7756
Fax. (804) 752-2163
www.revivalglory.org

10 1/2 Weeks of Summer Campmeeting 1998
Friday, June 26 through Labor Day, September 7
With three great services daily

*Ruth Heflin will be speaking nightly the first two
weeks of campmeeting*

Winter Campmeeting 1998
February 6 – March 1

Ruth Heflin will be speaking nightly the first week

*Ministry tapes and song tapes are also available
upon request.*

Mount Zion Miracle Prayer Chapel

13 Ragheb Nashashibi
P.O. Box 20897
Sheikh Jarrah
Jerusalem, Israel

Tel. 972-2-5828964
Fax. 972-2-5824725
www.revivalglory.org

Prayer Meetings:

2:00 – 3:00 P.M. Daily
Monday – Thursday

Services:
Friday, Saturday and Sunday
10:30 A.M.
7:30 P.M.
Pre-meeting praise 7:00 P.M.

Come and worship with us in Jerusalem!